GOLF

Bernard Gallacher has successfully combined the ultimate golf roles of international tournament player and top club professional*. As the winner of 20 titles in a competitive career spanning eight Ryder Cup team appearances, and resident professional at the renowned Wentworth Club which attracts golfers from all over the world, he is recognised as an outstanding teacher of the game.

Mark Wilson gained wide experience as the much-travelled golf writer of the Daily Express and London Evening Standard during his 32 years as a Fleet Street journalist. His writing has been published throughout the golf world, and his previous books include the official *PGA European Tour Guide to Better Golf* and *The Best of Henry Longhurst.*

*In 1989 he was appointed Captain of Europe's Ryder Cup.

TEACH YOURSELF BOOKS

'Golf is a science, the study of a lifetime, in which you may exhaust yourself but never your subject.'

David R. Forgan

GOLF

Bernard Gallacher
&
Mark Wilson

TEACH YOURSELF BOOKS

Hodder and Stoughton

First published 1988
Fifth impression 1990

Copyright © 1988
Bernard Gallacher and Mark Wilson

British Library Cataloguing in Publication Data
Gallacher, Bernard
Golf. – (Teach yourself books).
1. Golf – Manuals
I. Title   II. Wilson, Mark
796.352′3

ISBN 0 340 42294 7

Printed and bound in Great Britain
for Hodder and Stoughton Educational,
a division of Hodder and Stoughton Ltd,
Mill Road, Dunton Green, Sevenoaks, Kent,
by Clays Ltd, St Ives plc

Photoset by Rowland Phototypesetting Ltd,
Bury St Edmunds, Suffolk

This volume is available in the USA from
Random House, Inc.,
21 East 50th Street, New York, N.Y. 10022

Contents

Introduction

The appeal of golf has spread throughout the world to give enjoyment to many millions, and their numbers continue to grow each day. For all players the game provides a continual challenge to learn from one's mistakes. There are the comparative few who have developed an enviable talent to play the game exceedingly well. But the 'average golfer' can derive as much pleasure from his modest successes as the expert does from his mightier achievements, and it is this fact that begins to explain the true appeal of golf.

In the first instance, golf answers the need in everyone's nature to be competitive. Golf is all about competing and the game's unique handicapping system allows any novice playing to the best of his ability, a chance to give a champion a good match, even to beat him on occasions. It is this facet for bringing the beginner and the accomplished player together on equal terms that places golf apart from other sports. Through the ages a great many people have attempted to define the qualities of golf. Something like a century ago David R. Forgan, who came from the Scottish family of club makers, gave his interpretation and no better definition has been seen since. He wrote:

> 'Golf is a science, the study of a lifetime, in which you may exhaust yourself but never your subject.
> 'It is a contest, a dual or a melee, calling for courage, skill, strategy and self-control.
> 'It is a test of temper, a trial of honour, a revealer of character.
> 'It affords a chance to play the man, and act the gentleman.
> 'It means going into God's out of doors, getting close to nature, a fresh air exercise, a sweeping away of the mental cobwebs, genuine recreation of the tired tissues.

'It is a cure for care – an antidote to worry.

'It includes companionship with friends, social intercourse, opportunity for courtesy, kindliness and generosity to an opponent.

'It promotes not only physical health but moral force.'

Every golfer is his own referee

Quite simply, golf holds every type of challenge. And, of course, it is the game of a lifetime. It can be taken up at the age of six and enjoyed to eighty and beyond. It is a game that prospers all the more for the importance it places upon pride. The newest recruit to the game will share the pride and sense of satisfaction felt by an Open Champion, when he hits a good shot. A beginner may well tee up the ball and mis-hit it fifty times but eventually he hits a good shot and at that moment his sights are set for the future. He knows that he has it in him to do it, and the challenge is there to be met. Certainly, it is a great test of character and of honesty. Every golfer is his own referee and on this understanding the game has remained one of the most honourable of all sports.

The learning of golf lasts a lifetime, and always remains an unfinished exercise; the greatest golfers freely admit they are constantly learning something new each day, and Open champions are the first to declare that perfection in golf is an impossible dream. Improvement is a realistic challenge at all levels.

To succeed in this task means, in the beginning, a thorough learning of the fundamentals of the game and this, we must emphasise, is best done with a professional golfer. Lessons from a good teacher are invaluable to the novice, but once on the right road, you can start to teach yourself, and this book will help you progress swiftly in the right direction. Expert guidance as you first learn is essential, and without it you will almost certainly develop bad habits which will plague your golf and deny you full enjoyment of the game.

Tuition in itself is not enough, however. You must also do a great deal for yourself. Once you understand the fundamentals, then you can build on them – and that means many hours of working on the game alone. It is at this stage that you will find this book most helpful. Take it to the practice ground for immediate reference, and make efficient use of the material by concentrating on one section at a time.

Experiment to learn

The most effective way of learning is to experiment. The object is simple enough: to learn how to hit the ball consistently well enough to enjoy the game. Practice is an art in itself; it has to be carried out intelligently and with a prepared purpose. There is no sense hitting a hundred golf balls aimlessly. Little more is achieved that way than the exercising of muscles. When these tire, mistakes, bad habits and costly faults are built into the golf swing for future punishment. The golfer who practises intelligently will find his dedication neither dull or monotonous, but rewarding.

1

Choosing your Equipment

The equipment

When taking up the challenge of golf the choosing of the right equipment is as essential as it is simple. Take advice from a professionals' shop; mistakes are costly, and as bad tools will always create a bad workman, so will bad clubs produce a bad golfer.

The clubs

In the beginning there is absolutely no need to buy a full set of 14 clubs involving an outlay of hundreds of pounds. Seven clubs can suffice for a while, a 3 wood, then say, numbers 3, 5, 7, 9 irons, a sand wedge and a putter. (See Figure 1).

It is important to match the lies (determined by the angle between the clubhead and the shaft – see Figure 2, page 8) and the lofts (the angle of the clubface – see Figure 3, page 9) whatever number of clubs you choose to play do form a truly balanced set and not a collection of oddments. The same applies to a constant swing weight which gives each club an identical 'feel' in the hands. Considerable care has also to be taken in selecting the right flex and length of club shaft. It is just like putting an engine together – if one component is faulty then the rest have no chance of performing to their full potential.

Happily, the task of buying the right equipment is considerably easier now than it was some years ago when hickory shafts made the collection of a matched set a lifetime pursuit. Today, the manufacturers bear the burden and unless you are of extremely abnormal physique there is a factory-made product instantly suited to your needs. Even so, there is still the first hurdle to be surmounted: deciding exactly what it is that best suits you as an aspiring golfer.

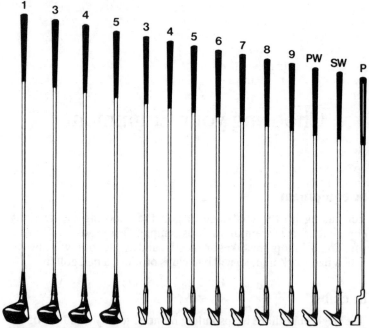

Fig. 1 A popular composition of a full set of 14 clubs. The maximum number allowed by the rules.
Left to right. Nos 1–5 woods, Nos 3–9 irons, pitching wedge, sand wedge and putter. As the loft increases, the length of the shaft decreases.

There are different ways to tackle this problem. The first is, naturally, to consult the professional at your golf club or driving range. He can give you the same attention and detailed advice as a tailor fitting you for an expensive suit. Some manufacturers are happy to lend, through club professionals, a sample of their products for use on the practice ground. In the same way that it would be most unwise to buy a new car without a test run, so the golfer seeking a set of clubs should insist on some form of trial to help him make his final choice.

If you have friends who are golfers already don't hesitate to ask them for a loan of their clubs before making a final choice. Again, if you are thinking of buying a second-hand set of clubs to get started – and there is absolutely nothing wrong in this – and your professional has something on offer, arrange to use them on a trial basis. Whatever you do, don't buy a set of expensive clubs simply because you like the look of them.

In the selection processs there are general guidelines to help. The shaft is the most important part of a club and there are a number of different designs with varying weights and flexes from which to choose. If you get it right, playing golf becomes much simpler; get it wrong and your struggles with unsuitable equipment will take the enjoyment out of the game quite quickly. As a generalisation, the stiffer the shaft the greater chance you have of hitting the ball straight. Increased flex to make the shaft 'whippy' is an aid to hitting the ball a greater distance. But it is not a simple matter. Your physique and temperament as a golfer play a large part in deciding which of the two shafts is best for you. If, for example you have comparatively weak hands, then the kind of stiff shafts used by tournament professionals will cause you nothing but trouble. They will have a stiff, 'poker' feeling and it will be impossible for you to achieve the all-essential clubhead speed throught the ball at impact. For an extreme example, try swinging a broom like a golf club and then a thin cane. Obviously, then cane will 'swish' through the air at a much faster rate. Conversely, if you have the natural asset of strong hands then a club that has a shaft with too much flex is the wrong choice. The tendency is to 'whip' the clubface out of line, and then the ball can go in any direction.

If your natural tendency is to rush through life, to run rather than walk, you are likely to have a fast swing, in which case you are more likely to find success with a heavier, stiffer club shaft. If you have a slow, smooth swing then the extra whip of a more flexible shaft should be considered. Discovering which of these many shafts is best suited to your needs is most effectively done by taking an hour on the practice ground with examples of each type.

Beware the temptation to tinker with the idea of having club shafts shorter or longer than standard. It may seem sound in theory, and it is a thought that comes to all beginners, but you really do have to be of unusual build to require the lengthening or shortening of shafts. The different needs of short and tall players is met through adjusting the lie of a club and that poses no problem to the professional who has a special gadget in his shop for that very purpose.

Attention to detail is never more important than when determining the thickness of the rubber or leather grips on your set of clubs. A youngster struggling with grips intended for an adult with large hands can develop bad habits that plague him for years; indeed, posture has a knock-on effect that can damage your whole game. Think carefully about every item of equipment. Do not be tempted

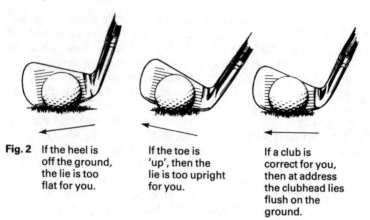

Fig. 2 If the heel is off the ground, the lie is too flat for you.

If the toe is 'up', then the lie is too upright for you.

If a club is correct for you, then at address the clubhead lies flush on the ground.

into starting with a straight faced (strong) driver in an attempt to power the ball prodigious distances from the tee. That comes later. The No. 3 wood with its customary 14 degrees of loft will best serve the learner. He needs a club that is going to help him sweep the ball into the air. Which particular irons to choose for a 'short' set is another matter of personal preference. Most beginners settle for the 3, 5, 7, 9, sand wedge and putter to go with their No. 3 wood. But there is nothing to say you shouldn't select the 4, 6, 8 and wedge as alternative irons. Figure 3 shows the average degrees of loft for normal woods and irons. What should be accepted is that seven clubs are enough for a start. They can always be 'matched up' later

	Club		
	No. 1	11 degrees	Driver
Woods	No. 3	14 degrees	3 Wood
	No. 4	19 degrees	4 Wood
	No. 5	23 degrees	5 Wood
	No. 2	20 degrees	
	No. 3	23 degrees	Long irons
	No. 4	27 degrees	
	No. 5	31 degrees	
	No. 6	35 degrees	Middle irons
	No. 7	39 degrees	
	No. 8	43 degrees	
	No. 9	47 degrees	Short irons
Pitching wedge		52 degrees	
Sand wedge		58 degrees	

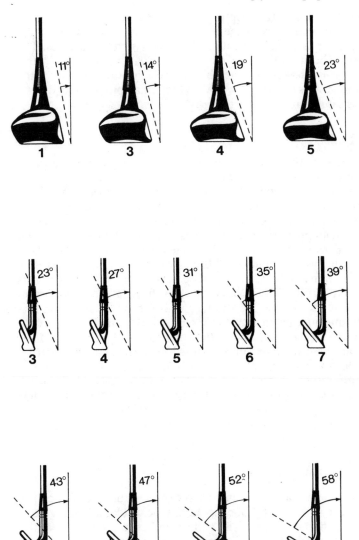

Fig. 3 Average degrees of loft for the most popular woods and irons.

to make a full set. In accepting this, there is absolutely no fear of feeling embarrassment when playing alongside others who may be carrying the full complement of 14 clubs allowed by the rules. The power of positive thinking plays a great part in golf and in this respect it is as well to remember that Harry Vardon, one of the greatest golfers in history, won the Open Championship six times – and he rarely carried more than seven clubs.

The balls

After making the right choice of clubs there is the importance of deciding which of the many brands and designs of golf ball on the market is right for you. The answer, again is very much a matter of personal preference, and what you can afford. There are four main alternatives beginning with the high compression ball favoured by tournament professionals. This has a thin Balata covering and inside there is another small ball filled with liquid wrapped in a seemingly endless band of rubber. The characteristics of this ball promote maximum distance and spin as an aid to controlling its fight. At impact, the comparatively soft Balata covering stays fractionally longer on the clubface. But for the same reason it is much, much easier to damage or 'cut' the ball and this can prove expensive for the beginner. At the other end of the range on offer is the solid ball, a composition of tough synthetic rubber materials resistant to damage. Inevitably, it is also resistant to spin and is therefore all the more difficult to control on hitting the ground. There is also what is known as the two-piece ball, a synthetic centre covered by Surlyn and a fourth type which has a wound centre covered by Surlyn, particularly recommended for novices as offering the best of all worlds.

Shoes and clothing

There are very many different kinds of golf shoe but the basic choice is between spikes and rubber soles. On the whole, the best golfers prefer traditional spikes. The golf swing has to be built on a firm base, with no slipping or sliding, and spikes most certainly answer this need. This is not to say, however, that the rubber-soled lighter golf shoe does not have its usefulness on a dry summer's day.

Clothing, naturally, is a matter of personal preference up to a point. You will probably find it a worthwhile investment to purchase a golfing sweater which provides a degree of waterproof protection.

As in any sport, your clothes should fit comfortably so as not to restrict your movements, but it should be recognised by every beginner that golfers pride themselves as being among the smartest of all sportsmen. This is not a matter of vanity – as you will find, the golfer who feels smart and tidy in his appearance will also tend to apply the same high standards to his game on the course.

2

Getting a Grip on the Game

The fundamentals of golf

By the fundamentals of golf we mean how to grip the club, stand to the ball properly, and how to groove the backswing and downswing into one finely balanced and co-ordinated movement of controlled power. The learning process will be greatly accelerated by watching others who are proficient at the game, especially the best tournament professionals.

It would be an act of kindness to deny any beginner the right to leave the practice ground for the golf course itself until he had made a habit of gripping the club correctly. There is no such thing as any one 'secret' to success in golf, but there is certainly a single factor which can guarantee perpetual trouble, and that is a bad grip. Among average golfers, only one in six, it is said, has anything like a proper grip, and this goes a considerable way to explaining the problems of the great majority. In fact, mastering a good grip is, basically, very simple, and if you take the trouble to learn this early on, you will have every chance to make the most of your ability, and enjoy the game as it should be enjoyed. Neglecting to acquire a good grip will condemn you to unceasing frustration. The right grip is the key to all progress; fail to recognise this and you will spend your whole golfing life trying to compensate for it. In turn, compensations lead to the development of the wrong arm muscles, and after a while, it is difficult, perhaps even impossible, to make amends. So, getting it right at the start is imperative.

The observance of several golden rules is required to acquire a grip that will not only allow but actively encourage a good swing and successful golf. Firstly, it has to be understood that although the club is 'held in the hands', it is actually gripped by the fingers of the right hand and the palm of the left. Often, too much emphasis is placed upon power in golf, and too little is thought about 'feel' and 'touch' which are equally important. The big muscles of the arms, shoulders and legs can generate most of the energy needed to power the shot, while the sensitive fingers bring the critical factor of 'feel' into play.

The next golden rule to understand, learn and practise until its observance becomes second nature, is that the two hands must work as a single unit. They should be equal partners, sharing their workload; if one dominates then the whole balance of the swing is destroyed, and you have a guaranteed recipe for turning a game of golf into a perpetual search for the ball.

The techniques of the grip

As shown in Figure 4, there are three basic methods from which the beginner can choose: the *Vardon* grip, the *interlocking* and the *double-handed* (often referred to as the *baseball* grip).

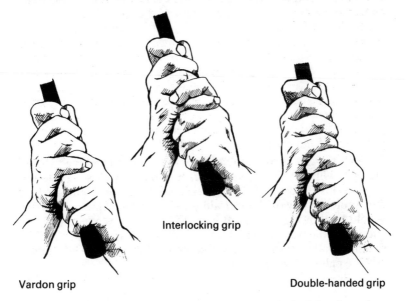

Interlocking grip

Vardon grip

Double-handed grip

Fig. 4 Three methods with the same objective; to make both hands work as one unit.

The Vardon grip

This is the most popular by far and it is to be recommended to all with normal-sized hands. Place the left hand on the shaft of the club so that it lies on a diagonal line running from the middle joint of the first finger to about an inch above the little finger, so nestling under the muscular pad of the palm (Figure 5). Close the fingers as if shaking hands, ensure that the V formed by the thumb and forefinger is pointing midway between the chin and right shoulder, and that part of the grip has been perfected (Figure 6).

The next move is to hold the club in the fingers of the right hand (Figures 7 and 8) which is then wrapped over the left so that the palm covers the left thumb. The little finger slides into the groove between the left forefinger and the middle finger, and the other three fingers of the right hand grip the club. Again, the V of the right hand should be pointing slightly right of the chin. The right forefinger should feel as though the top joint is gently squeezing the trigger.

When the grip is right, the back of the left hand and the palm of the right will both, along with the face of the club, be square to the target. This is absolutely essential. Another basic requirement is that preferably two, and certainly no more than three, knuckles should be showing on the left hand. This promotes a 'neutral' grip and opens the way to consistent, good golf (Figures 9 and 10). The pressure points in the hand should be felt between the left thumb and the palm of the right hand.

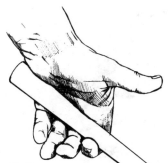

Fig. 5

Fig. 6

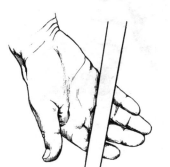

Fig. 7

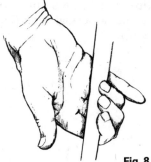

Fig. 8

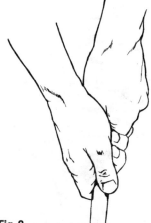

Fig. 9

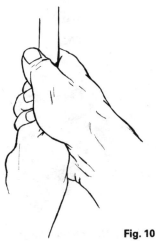

Fig. 10

The interlocking grip and double-handed grip

The alternative *interlocking* grip, good for those with short fingers and the *double-handed* grip, which can be helpful for lady golfers, juniors or men with small and weak hands, are no bar to playing golf well. Indeed, some of the best golfers in the history of the game have employed these methods. But in doing so they have religiously observed the basic essentials of the Vardon grip – both hands uniting to work together as a single unit (Figures 11–13).

Fig. 11   Vardon grip.

Fig. 12   Interlocking grip.

Fig. 13   Double-handed grip.

Even the best and most correct of grips can be ruined if the club is held too tightly or too loosely. Tightness promotes tension, and if the club is held so loosely that it slips in the hands then that is equally disastrous. The answer is to grip the club firmly in both hands, but not so strongly that the forearm muscles tighten to create tension. Aim for the same degree of pressure you would use to hold and throw a ball.

Fig. 14 'Normal' grip: V pointing between chin and right shoulder.

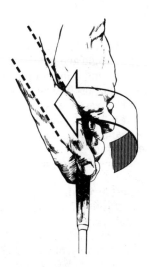

Fig. 15 'Strong' grip: both hands turned too far right, showing four knuckles of left hand.

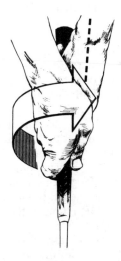

Fig. 16 'Weak' grip: both hands turned too far left, showing no knuckles on left hand.

3

Think before you Swing

The fascination of the golf swing has already withstood some 500 years of technical study, and it may well do so for as long again. Expert research has provoked a barrage of countless theories on how best to master the complexities of the swing, and yet ironically nothing could be simpler than its objective. All that is required of it is to deliver the clubface to the ball, square to the line of target, and with just the right amount of power to project it the required distance.

As a beginner you do not need to involve yourself in the advanced technicalities of the golf swing, indeed, you should avoid doing so at all cost. Otherwise, you will, as we say, become 'fouled up in the mechanics of the game' and fail to recognise that basically, when approached in the correct manner, golf is essentially a simple challenge. If you restrict your curiosity for a start to gaining a good understanding of the fundamentals of the game, then you will safely build the foundation for a lifetime of enjoyment.

An hour or two spent studying the methods of champions on the course as they play under pressure, answering both the physical and mental challenges of the game at the highest level, offer a priceless lesson without cost. It will also quickly help you to understand that there is no such thing as the one perfect golf swing.

While the outstanding players all observe the fundamentals, they have their own individual styles, largely dictated by physique. For example, a player of over six feet will swing the club in a different manner to a golfer of stockier build. So, if you wish to learn by imitation, and many thousands of newcomers do so quite success-fully, it is obviously wise to study someone whose physique is similar to your own.

Develop a mental picture

What should we be looking for when we study a professional on the golf course? For a start, particular note should be taken of how he carefully thinks about the objective of the shot he is about to make before even addressing the ball. The complete golf swing takes only about two seconds, so there really is no time to think during it. The good golfer will develop a *mental picture* of the shot he wants to hit. The object is to put the ball into the easiest position for the next shot, and he will be putting positive thoughts to work to make sure that this is done. A great golf swing is no help unless it is supported by good course strategy.

Fig. 17

Fig. 18

Addressing the ball

Once having settled on his objective
the expert stands to the ball and **ad-
dresses** it in a relaxed manner.

The head is cocked slightly to the
right so that he is looking at the back of
the ball, and it remains steady throughout the entire swing. It is impossible
to overemphasize the importance of
keeping the head steady. You must
overcome the temptation to watch the
clubhead on the takeaway for this leads
to a sway and complete loss of balance.

Fig. 19

The backswing

This is a co-ordinated movement of the hands, shoulders, hips and
legs. The left knee points to a spot behind the ball, the hips turn 45°,
the shoulders a full 90° so that the back is now pointing towards the
target; the left arm is kept firm and smoothness is the key to the
whole movement. There is no snatching of the clubface away from
the ball. When the turn is properly completed, then the clubhead
will also be aimed at the target.

Fig. 20   **Fig. 21**

The downswing

This is triggered by a slight lateral movement of the hips and a pulling down of the arms. Then a lively use of the hands together with a turning of the hips at impact allows the clubface to meet the back of the ball at maximum power. Success does not depend on brute force, but on timing, to achieve top speed precisely at impact.

If you think of the golf swing as a gear change in a car then it helps to understand what is wanted. Bottom gear is maintained for a smooth takeaway and after a short pause at the top of the swing the higher gears come into use as acceleration is built up to give the clubhead the power it needs.

All this energy has to be generated smoothly. The expert does not rush, he controls his power. In the beginning, it does no harm to try and swing back and down at the same speed. This will encourage smoothness, and the law of gravity will automatically quicken the downswing for you.

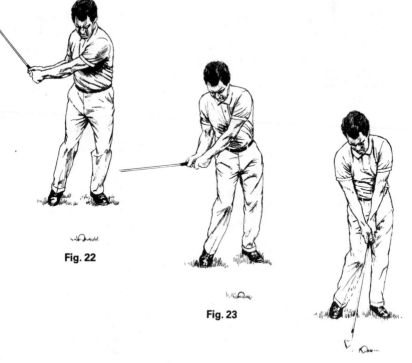

Fig. 22

Fig. 23

Fig. 24

The follow-through

Do not underestimate the importance of the follow-through, for it is just as much a part of the whole co-ordinated exercise as the initial takeaway. The head remains steady, the body balanced, and after keeping the clubface square to the target through the ball, the hands respond to the momentum of the shot and turn over. A really good golf swing leads eventually to a poised and elegant position at the finish.

Fig. 25

Fig. 26

Fig. 27

Recognise your limitations

It has been claimed often enough, by both the best and the worst of golfers, that the game is a more of a mental challenge than a physical test of ability. We believe the two departments to be of equal importance, but accept that the first essential when stepping onto a golf course is to appreciate your own limitations. All too often the average golfer will wreck his score, ruin his day, deny himself a prize, give victory to an opponent, with one careless, ill conceived shot. All too often he forgets his limitations, and attempts a shot that is not only beyond his own capabilities, but one which would be shunned even by an Open champion as being too adventurous.

Frequently, we see the best of tournament professionals, once having got into serious trouble, playing sideways to reach the safety of the fairway. But it is not uncommon to see the average golfer, faced with a similar problem, attempting a recovery of near miraculous proportions. He feels some compulsion to hit the ball forward, even when there is a virtual forest barring his way. He pays dearly for this bravado and lack of thought. It is absolutely essential to *think ahead*, visualise the next shot, determine in your mind where you need to hit the ball to make that one easier. Golf strategy, or course management as it is becoming better known, has been likened to a game of chess, each move fitting into a pattern of success. You will never become a good golfer, never even play to a modest handicap with consistency, unless you understand and accept your limitations.

To meet this need you have to be in the right frame of mind from the start, and that means avoiding arriving at the club with no time to spare and having to rush to the first tee. Always allow fifteen minutes at least for a gentle warming up. Why risk three hours of enjoyment on the course for the want of a little practice? Thirty balls with a wedge, gently working up to a full swing, can suffice. A few chips and a little putting will help to take away tension. All the time work on the fundamentals.

Nervousness on the first tee is inevitable if you have no idea what is going to happen when you swing. It is what you deserve if you have not bothered to go to the practice ground and rid yourself of this fear by going through the same process that you will face on the tee. Adopt a drill, follow a set routine, and you will find that it is a great antidote to nerves. Establish a pattern – the same number of practice swings before each shot, the same waggle of the clubhead to release tension, the same time spent addressing the ball before takeaway. This can be especially important.

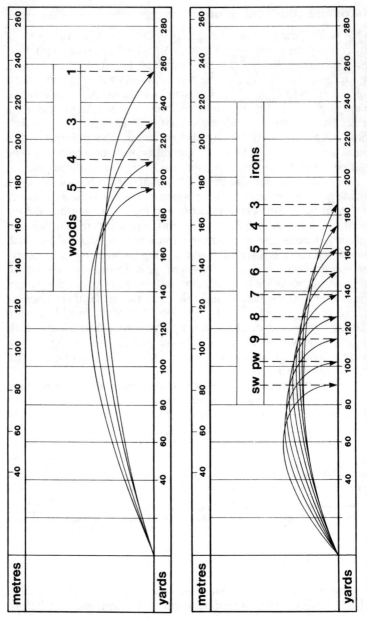

Fig. 28 Yardage chart showing distances possible in helpful conditions for average golfers with woods and irons.

Consistency and confidence are like the chicken and the egg in posing the question of which comes first. Certainly, good golf cannot be played without them. The one certain thing is that both are bred on the practice ground. Every golfer should know how far he is naturally capable of hitting the ball with each club in the bag and he must develop the consistency to achieve that distance every time. The chart on page 24 shows the normal distances achieved with the different clubs by the average golfer.

4

The Address

The correct 'set up' in golf, a combination of ball position, aim, stance and posture, requires a routine drill which the golfer ignores at his peril. It is the basis for success, or – for those who fail to make a meticulous habit of observing its importance – a certain cause of every conceivable form of bad shot. Quite frequently, on the practice ground at a major tournament, you will see one top professional having his set up drill checked by another. The very best players invariably recognise its vital bearing in determining how well they perform on the course. Unfortunately, not all average golfers share the same understanding. They will spend hours experimenting with their swings in the search for an answer to a problem when, most likely, the fault lies in the set up and a few seconds is all that is required to determine the answer.

In the set up position, the golfer is exactly like the marksman sighting his rifle. You must get it right, or miss the target. There is no room for carelessness, or for undue haste in wanting to 'pull the trigger' and hit the ball. Certainly, a few moments more spent in perfecting the address, can save five minutes of searching in the woods afterwards. There can be no argument with the fact that the way you set up has a direct bearing on the way you will swing the club. Most bad shots are created at the address position long before the swing starts, and the expert professional can estimate with reasonable accuracy the handicap of an amateur merely by watching him stand to the ball. Which leads to one of the truest sayings in golf – there has never yet been a good golfer with a bad set up, or a really bad golfer with a good set up.

We will begin with the ball position. The first, best suited to the kind of conditions encountered on most European golf courses, requires the ball to be positioned equidistant between the heels of the feet when playing the short irons, from the number 8 down to the sand wedge. As the clubs lengthen to meet the call for longer shots, so the position of the ball changes. The medium irons, numbers 7, 6 and 5, need the ball to be mid-way between the left heel and the centre of the body. At the same time the feet are gradually being placed wider apart. The long irons, the fairway woods and the driver call for the ball to be opposite or just inside the left heel, and the spacing of your feet will match the width of your shoulders.

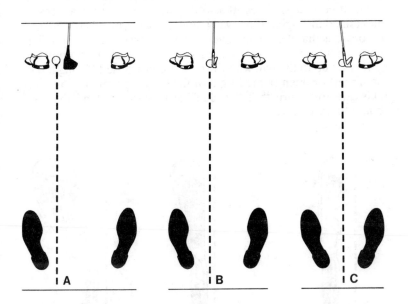

Fig. 29 Ball position at address for:
   A Driver, fairway   **B** Medium irons   **C** Short irons
   woods, long irons

The second method, favoured for golf courses where the grass is in a lush condition, calls for the ball to be played opposite or just inside the left heel for all shots. The feet are placed about six inches apart for the wedge, but while the ball remains in a constant position, the right foot is moved further to the right progressively for the longer clubs, until on reaching the driver, the width is again equal to that of the shoulders.

Aim with the care of a marksman

The importance of the aim – the correct alignment of the clubface at the address – must be obvious. Again, it is just like the sharp-shooter marksman sighting his rifle onto the bulls-eye of the target. You should take great care to place the clubface behind the ball, square to the line of your intended shot. A good many average golfers mistakenly hurry their way through the process, place the club down in a more or less square position, and trust that some compensation through instinct will correct any error in the down-swing. It very rarely does. If as little as a 1° error at the address is maintained throughout the swing, and the ball is hit 200 yards, then it is obvious that it is going to miss the target by a wide margin. The more solidly the ball is struck the greater the punishment. Only bad golfers set up to the ball with the clubface in a closed (facing left of the target) or open (aimed right of the target) position. You must take care to ensure that the clubface is placed behind the ball, square to the target.

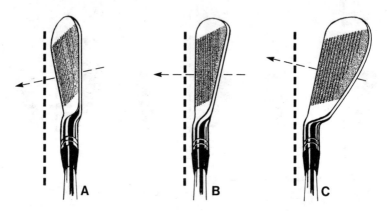

Fig. 30 **A** *Closed* clubface –   **B** *Square* clubface.   **C** *Open* clubface –
ball will start left   ball will start right.

A common and costly mistake made by many beginners when using irons, is to square the top edge of the blade to the ball and line of target. So take care to line up with the *bottom* or *leading edge* of the club. The top edge of the club should point to the right of the target.

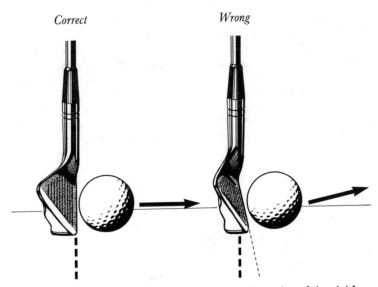

Correct   *Wrong*

Fig. 31 Be sure to line up with the bottom or leading edge of the clubface square to the target – *not* the top edge.

To achieve the correct stance and body alignment demanded for a square set up it is helpful to imagine playing golf on a railway line. When the club is placed behind the ball, aimed at the target, the feet, knees, hands, hips and shoulders are all running parallel to the intended line of the shot. The left arm and the shaft of the club need to be in a reasonably straight line, comfortably straight for flexibility is essential, and the right arm has to be slightly bent with the elbow pointing towards the front of the right hip.

Fig. 32 To achieve the correct set-up routine, imagine playing golf on a railway line.

You should, as you are learning, concentrate on the 'square set up' approach to golf. There are variations (see Figure 33), but these are best left alone until you are thoroughly equipped with the fundamental techniques. Then, you can with justification experiment in a great many directions, for outside of the fundamentals there is nothing absolutely rigid in golf. There is no one way to play the game. A day at a tournament, spent watching the very best professionals, will make this very plain. It is all a matter of finding out by experiment which variations most help your game.

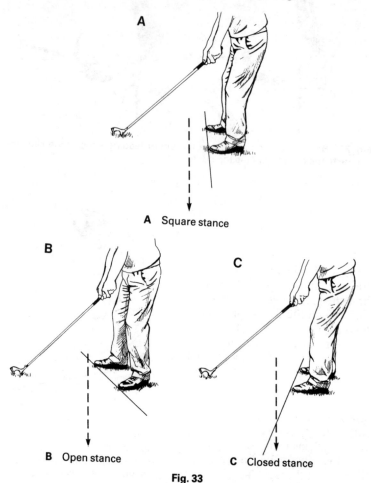

A Square stance

B Open stance

C Closed stance

Fig. 33

Golf demands a turning or rotation of the body and free swing of the arms and hands, and for this a good posture is essential. The first requirement is to stand the correct distance from the ball at the address position. The simplest aid to determine this is to stand to the ball, and lower the club until the butt end of the grip touches the left leg about two inches above the knee. Then bend forward from the hips, taking care to keep the back straight. Do not crouch; to become cramped at the address is to deny the hands and arms any chance of swinging freely. Stand proud, hold your head up, do not let your chin drop down onto your chest, as this can only impair the movement of your shoulders, causing them to lift instead of turning on a flat plane. Bad positioning of the head will also prevent a full pivot.

Hold the chin up and the head steady to allow the shoulders to turn freely for a full pivot.

Fig. 34 Incorrect address position.   **Fig. 35** Correct address position.

Your knees should be flexed forward and inwards, and the weight needs to be evenly distributed between your feet for good balance and mobility. Your head position is also extremely important in maintaining a balance. It should, at the address, be behind a line drawn vertically up from the ball, and it should stay there throughout the entire swing (Figure 35). A steady head position is necessary to allow a full, free swing; but 'steady' does not mean holding it rigidly still. To be rigid is to create tension, and tension is always an obstacle to good golf. It makes a correct posture, which dictates a golfer's swing plane, quite impossible. So the message to remember is: stand proud to the ball, feel relaxed and comfortable, keep the head behind the ball and steady.

5

The Backswing

As you try to meet the challenge of playing consistently to the limit of your ability, to enjoy the pleasures of the game to the full, you can be greatly helped at any stage by pausing to develop a clear mental picture of the immediate objective. You will find this especially true at the start of the backswing – the all important takeaway movement based on a rhythmic, balanced, highly co-ordinated and power-generating use of the body. If any one unit – arms, hands, legs, hips, shoulders, head – fails to do its duty, then trouble looms. They must work together like a well rehearsed relay team. Rather than try to think of each component part and seriously risk confusion, you will benefit from concentrating on just two primary thoughts. You should start the backswing with the picture of a slowly revolving door in your mind. This will give you a mental image of what you are trying to imitate, and convey a sense of the smoothness and rhythm to be achieved. Then on the completion of the backswing you can visualise your body as a tightly coiled spring held under control and ready to unleash its energy.

A modest waggle of the clubhead or forward press with the hands to relieve tension, starts the backswing. The hands are the great dictators in golf, through them all the muscles of the body are put to work, the clubhead answers to their every command, and so they must be kept active. The takeaway has been called 'the most important eighteen inches in golf' and has prompted a multitude of theories. It is essential in the early stages, however, to simplify your task as much as possible, and you can do this by concentrating on a one-piece movement to waist level. The feeling you have to develop is one of the hands, arms, shoulders and clubhead moving as one unit.

Fig. 36 The backswing turns the body into a powerful coil.

Fig. 37 The first 18 inches of the backswing dictate everything that follows.

When the clubhead is at waist level, the clubface should still be 'square' to your body which has started to pivot, and the same number of knuckles on the left hand will be visible as at the address position. While the arms swing around and upwards the shoulders turn on as flat a plane as possible.

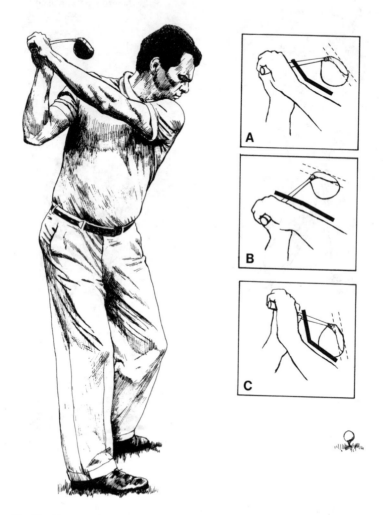

Fig. 38   Keep the clubface 'square (**A**) throughout the backswing, rather than closed (**B**) or open (**C**).

Fig. 39 The club should go no further than parallel with the ground.

Turn the shoulders on a flat plane – never tilt them.

Settle for comfort

Many of the requirements of the backswing are supplied by nature. The coiling of the upper part of the body will force the hips to turn through the necessary 45°, and the left knee, helped by a slight raising of the left heel, will co-operate in turn by pointing to a spot behind the ball. Ideally, the pivot continues until a firm left arm has the hands head high, the club shaft parallel to the ground, and the shoulders at 90° so that the back now faces the target. This, it has to be accepted, demands a state of athletic suppleness which is not common to all beginners; so it should be remembered that more harm is done by straining to reach a position that is uncomfortable, than by settling for a restricted swing.

It is still quite possible to play excellent golf with a three-quarter swing and several top tournament professionals have proved this point. Do not make the common mistake of thinking that the clubhead should be taken straight back from the ball, on an extension of the target line, and then brought back to impact point in the same way. The golf swing does not allow this to happen; for it to be possible, your body would have to be bent forward at the address so that your spine was parallel to the ground. The successful golfer must have the image of a rounded golf swing, and the mental picture of a revolving door best provides it.

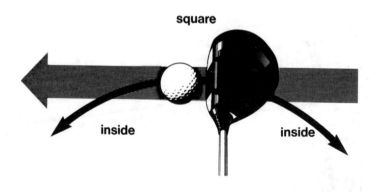

Fig. 40   A good swing delivers the clubhead from the inside to square to the inside again.

Your left arm must be kept as firm as possible throughout the backswing, and as your right arm bends, its elbow should be kept reasonably close to your body. At the top of the backswing, your left shoulder will brush your chin. It cannot be stressed too strongly, that throughout the whole of the co-ordinated movement of the body, your head position must remain steady. If the head moves the arc of the swing will change, and when that happens the chances of bringing the clubface back squarely to the ball are remote. During the backswing, your weight is transferred naturally and gradually to the right foot. Do not worry about when and how your wrists should be cocked; nature will take its course and they will behave accordingly.

Fig. 41 For a full drive, 75% of the body weight should be on the inside of the right foot at completion of the backswing.

While there is no one ideal swing plane for all golfers, the position of the clubface at the top of the backswing should be common to all. It should not be too 'open' with the toe pointing towards the ground or too 'closed' with the clubface looking at the sky, but 'square', halfway between the two, with the clubface at 45° and the shaft aimed directly at the target. The rhythm of the backswing is dictated by two words – slow and smooth. The vast majority of beginners swing far too quickly and very rarely do we see one who does not need to slow down.

38 *Golf*

Fig. 42(i) Three different positions of the clubhead at the top of the swing: **A** open (with the toe pointing towards the ground; **B** closed (with the clubface towards the sky; **C** square. You should be square at the top of the swing.

WRONG

WRONG

CORRECT

Fig. 42(ii) Three different alignments of the club shaft at the top of the swing: **A** pointing left of the target; **B** pointing right of the target; and **C** pointing at the target. **C** is correct.

A

WRONG

B

WRONG

C

CORRECT

A persistent problem for those learning the game, and one which you must cure at an early stage, comes from allowing the hips to move to the right with a lateral movement instead of turning during the takeaway. Any tendency to sway in this manner can be corrected with another mental picture. Imagine that you are swinging inside a barrel. The only way to avoid scraping the inside is to turn your hips properly.

Fig. 43 To avoid the dangers of swaying, imagine that you are swinging inside a barrel.

Tilting your shoulders instead of turning them on a flat plane is equally harmful. A good practice routine for this department of the game is to stand with your feet together while hitting with medium irons. It compels a correct turning of the body – otherwise loss of balance would cause you to fall off the shot. Remember too that the grip must be kept firm throughout. At the top of the swing you should be gripping the club just as firmly as you were at the address position. A simple practice-ground aid is to place a scorecard between the top joints of the two thumbs. If it falls out during the backswing then the hands are not working together.

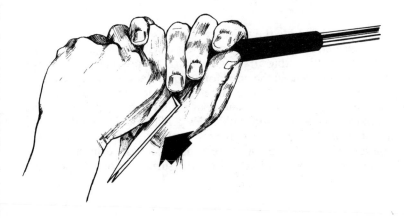

Fig. 44 The left thumb is directly under the shaft at the top of the backswing, and the grip should be just firm enough to hold a scorecard in place as a practice-ground exercise.

6

The Downswing and Follow-through

Scientists who study the physical demands of golf with the use of sophisticated robots and timing devices can make the playing of the game seem a daunting affair. They delight in proving that once the golfer has recognised the need for a momentary pause at the top of the backswing, and then committed himself to attacking the ball, he has only one fifth of a second to get it all right by delivering the clubface at a speed of some 100 miles per hour to a precisely square point of impact. In effect, however, the downswing is a simple matter, which calls for the observance of a basic drill in order to allow nature to take its course through a succession of reflex actions.

Fig. 45   The clubhead travels along an inside-square-inside path.

The first essential of the drill is to understand clearly the principles of the 'inside to out, and then inside again' arc of the downswing. Obviously, at the top of the swing the clubhead is inside the line to the target, having been taken to that position by the pivoting of the body. Now the challenge is to return the clubface to the ball on the same line as the backswing, and in such a manner that at the exact moment of impact it will be square, thus precisely duplicating its position at the point of address. Then, if the right balance is maintained, the controlled momentum of the swing will carry the clubhead back inside the line for the follow-through to complete the in-to-in arc of the swing (see Figure 45).

A brief pause at the top before starting the process of attacking the ball, is helpful. It is a safeguard against 'starting down' before completing the backswing properly. Failure to complete a full pivot is one of the most persistent problems for beginners. Any curtailing of the shoulder turn on the way back will encourage the clubhead to be taken back on an outside arc resulting in an out-to-in swing path with the clubface cutting across the ball and creating all kinds of trouble. Golf then becomes an awfully difficult game, whereas the correct positioning of the body at the top of the swing makes the rest so much simpler.

The one fifth of a second it takes to reach the point of impact allows only one constructive swing thought. We suggest that this should be concerned with starting the downswing with a slight lateral movement of the hips – a slide of about six centimetres to the left, parallel to the target line, and a tugging down of the arms. Done properly, this movement works like a key in unlocking the rest of the body from its fully coiled state at the top. It sets the correct angle of attack, and initiates the transfer of weight back to the left side. Trying to think of all the component parts of the downswing is to invite disaster. Concentrate on getting that first initial hip movement right and a fair degree of 'auto pilot' will take over. As your arms and the hands pull down together with the shifting of your hips, the coil unwinds. After the slide, your hips begin to turn, so establishing the inside arc of the downswing. The hips and arms are the leaders in the downswing, everything else follows to their command. This combination is a safeguard against your right shoulder throwing the club across the line. 'Hitting from the top' as it is sometimes mistakenly called guarantees the clubhead approaching the ball from across the target line.

Fig. 46 A slight sideways thrust of the hips triggers the down-swing with a downward pull of the arms . . .

Fig. 47 . . . and guides the way to the correct position at impact. The weight is transferred to the left side of the body, hips now turned, head still steady behind the ball and clubface square to the target.

You must resist the urge to attack the ball from the top of the swing with the upper body only. Unfortunately, it is a very easy trap to fall into, often stemming from an obsession with 'power', trying to hit the ball a maximum distance, which may mislead you into throwing your right shoulder into the action instead of starting the whole downward movement with a slight lateral shift of the hips and then a co-ordinated turning of the hips and free swing of the arms. There is no sense in achieving a good, smooth backswing and then lunging at the ball. While creating energy, the downswing also has to be controlled, balanced, and geared to a rhythm that will allow maximum power to be reached at the point of impact. Essential to this is keeping the head back behind the ball until well after impact. Unnecessary movement of the head is the first step towards swaying, and will inevitably ruin your swing.

Fig. 48 The head must stay behind the ball throughout the swing.

Allow nature to help

As in the backswing, do not become obsessed with thinking about when and how to un-cock the wrists. Let nature take care of it for a start, any little refinements in the search for added power can be taken care of at a later stage. At this point, you should restrict yourself to doing what is simplest. You will come to no harm by concentrating upon the thought that your hands do not begin to unleash the power in the downswing until they have come into what is called the hitting area, the last third of the downward arc. The primary object is to create a swing of gradual acceleration, timed to reach maximum velocity at the moment of impact.

Again, it can be extremely helpful to study a top tournament professional. Notice how he will seemingly hit the ball with half the explosive energy used by the average golfer – and yet send it half as far again.

The ultimate objective is to swing the clubhead *through* the ball and to achieve this it is helpful to think of swinging the clubhead down the target line for a couple of feet after impact. This is not literally possible, of course – the turning of the body so that the chest is facing the target, or even slightly left of it, must bring the clubhead back inside the line. But it is a thought process, and another mental picture, that encourages good timing of the shot. You may understandably question the importance of the follow-through, on the grounds that once having hit the ball and sent it on its way to the target, there is nothing you can do to influence the path of its flight. But you will soon learn that what comes after impact has a real meaning on the golf swing. A stylish, balanced finish with the arms extended through the ball for the hands to finish high, and with the left side of the body bearing all the weight, becomes a meaningful judgement of all the good that has been done before. The basic drills of the downswing have to be observed and carried out if the follow-through is to be successfully completed. Once impact has been achieved, the 'down, under and through' process of the shoulders continues as the body rotates, the right hand climbs over the left at the limit of extension, the right knee continues to move in towards the left, the head, held steady for so long, is at last allowed to come up with the arms, and if the balance is right, the process of gradual deceleration will lead to a neat and tidy finish. Then, hopefully, comes the time to enjoy the satisfaction of a well struck shot that has resulted from a successful appreciation that good golf is dependent upon a rhythmic swinging of the arms, and a balanced transference of weight.

Fig. 49 Good balance must be maintained for a poised finish to the swing.

Fig. 50 Swing the clubhead *through* the ball, and then let the hands roll over naturally.

Fig. 51   The good golfer at his best can come close to the perfection of the robot.

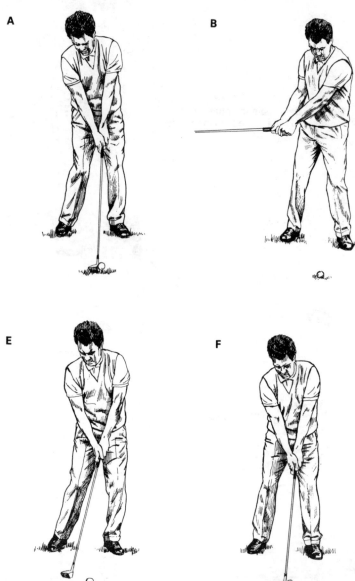

C

D

G

H

7

The Driver, Fairway Woods
and Irons

There is no question about which shot consistently offers the greatest satisfaction in golf; nothing can compare with the pleasure of hitting a straight and powerful drive from the tee. But the beginner's quest for this ultimate enjoyment requires a sound understanding of the basic techniques involved. Otherwise, initial failures can swiftly lead to a feeling of intimidation, and the tee is essentially a place for confidence, not negative thoughts. It is common to hear a golfer complain that he has always been a poor, or at best, indifferent driver of the ball. Those who fail to learn well at the start inevitably develop bad habits which become increasingly difficult to cure.

The first requirement is to show the driver itself the respect it deserves. A combination of straight face – usually 11° in loft – and long shaft – the standard length is forty-three inches – makes it the most difficult club to master. On the other hand, however, there is the compensation of being able to put the ball on a tee peg for a perfect lie every time the driver is used from the tee. Even so, it is wise for the beginner to accept that the driver can create problems in the early learning stages. No satisfaction can be gained by using it to hit the ball a prodigious distance, if it is then lost in trees either side of the fairway.

There is no disgrace, but considerable wisdom, in first gaining confidence on the tee by using a No. 3 wood, sometimes still referred to as a spoon, which has a clubface loft of around 14°. Obviously, this makes hitting the ball up and into the air much easier. The concession of something like 30 yards in distance is a small sacrifice to make for the reward of accuracy. When consistency has been achieved this way, then the driver can be tackled with confidence.

The first step in developing a good driving technique is to make sure to *tee up* the ball properly. It should be placed on the tee peg at a height that ensures half the ball showing above the face of the driver at the address position, and as already explained, it should be approximately in line with the left heel. A slight variation is permissible to meet personal needs. For example, if you tend to slice, you may find it helpful to move the ball back an inch or so.

Fig. 52 The correct height for teeing up the ball for a drive.

Fig. 53 The correct teeing-up position.

The swing demanded by the use of the driver is simply the basic swing. But because of the power and distance factors involved, strict observance of the fundamentals is never more important. Rhythm and clubhead speed are the critical requirements, and this is the time to be aware of the fact that power is not so much about hitting the ball hard, but striking it well. Beware the temptation to strain for extra momentum by rushing the swing. The need, now more than ever, is to swing smoothly, making the fullest possible pivot, transferring seventy-five per cent of the weight to the right side on the backswing and then back to the left on the way down, and only then speeding the hands through the impact zone. The objective is to have the clubface make contact with the ball slightly on the upswing with a sweeping action. The drive with a wood club has to be a sweep, unlike that with the irons which call for a slightly downward angle of attack.

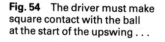

Fig. 54 The driver must make square contact with the ball at the start of the upswing . . .

. . . while the irons strike the ball on the downswing, thus achieving greater backspin.

The whole secret of good driving is to have a mental picture of the clubhead sweeping the ball off the tee peg to fly high. But while observing the demands of technique, do not overlook the strategy that has to be applied to every drive. The primary aim is to hit the ball from the tee to a position on the fairway that makes the next shot towards the green as simple as possible.

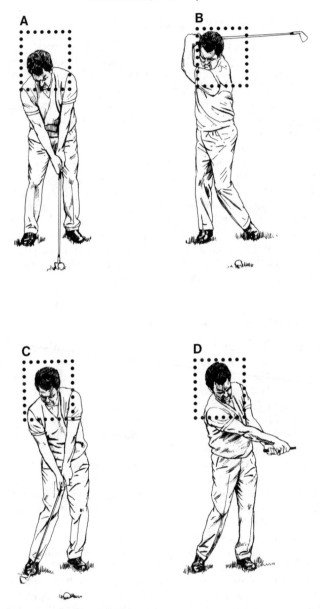

Fig. 55 Keep the head steady throughout the swing.

The fairway woods – think 'smooth'

The ability to consistently play good fairway wood shots rests largely on allowing the loft of the club face to do the work for which it has been designed. You must overcome any urge to try and scoop the ball into the air. Once again, all you have to do is to sweep the clubhead through the impact zone and allow the loft of each club to work. More than ever, the mental picture has to be of a smooth, slow start to the backswing, keeping the clubhead low to the ground for the first 18″ or so. Keep thinking 'smooth', for the fairway wood shot is a sweeping action, not an aggressive attacking of the ball. Remember, there is *no substitute for accuracy* in golf. Ideally, the ball position for fairway wood shots is just inside the left heel. But when faced with a poor lie, moving it back an inch or two towards the centre of the stance can help. While enjoying that amount of freedom of choice, be sure to observe religiously the basic laws – swing smoothly, make a full pivot, sweep through with balance and rhythm, and never force it. A controlled swing is of paramount importance when using the fairway wood.

The long irons – aim for a 'pinching' effect

Iron play is essentially about accuracy, but the first lesson to be learned has to do with distance. Good scoring will always be dependent upon successful club selection, and the importance of this facet of the game has been recognised to the extent that no top tournament professional is likely to go on the course without his yardage chart. The beginner also has to know the maximum distance he can hit with each iron. Such knowledge automatically builds consistency and confidence into his game. It is very difficult indeed to concentrate on making a sound swing if the mind is filled with doubt about whether the right club has been chosen for the task. Playing the long irons, Nos 2, 3, and 4 – with clubface lofts ranging from 20° to 27° – will give you more problems than any other area of the game. You would be wise for a start to leave the No 2 iron well alone for it demands a degree of expertise that can only come with experience. To begin with, an understanding is required of the main difference between hitting the tee shot and an iron. The drive, as we have explained, calls for the ball to be swept into the air as the clubhead starts upwards. But the purpose of the iron shot is to make a downward contact – the clubface striking the ball first and then the turf in front of it just as it reaches the lowest point in the arc of its downswing. A 'pinching' effect is created and the loft of the club imparts backspin on the ball and this in turn helps it to 'brake' to a halt on coming to earth. The need to hit down should not be allowed to develop into a chopping swing, however. The same *basic* principles apply in general to long irons as for the woods.

The ball should be positioned a shade inside the left heel and the feet must be comfortably far enough apart to provide the solid base needed for a successful partnership between balance and power. The requirement is to hit down on the back of the ball and to help this, your hands must be slightly ahead of the ball at the point of address. At impact, this position will be duplicated, the hands leading the clubhead as part of the more pronounced down-and-through swing pattern essential for iron shots. Swing well within yourself, concentrating on rhythm. Never try to scoop the ball; always have confidence that the loft of the club will get the ball airborne.

The medium irons – use the power of positive thinking

So often, the medium irons are the making or the breaking of a good score. They offer the accuracy needed to attack with confidence. To make the most of the opportunity a routine becomes necessary. Establish a set pattern, make a habit of creating a mental picture of the shot that is needed before addressing the ball. The power of positive thinking is sometimes stronger than the physical strength of the body muscles. When you are clear in your mind about what is wanted, then stand to the ball, pick a spot a few inches in front of it – a weed, an old divot mark, or whatever – that is on the target line and use this as an aiming aid for making sure that the clubface is set square. If you go through this procedure each time, knowing how far it is to the target and that you have selected the right club, then the anxiety is taken out of the shot.

The short irons – hit firmly and cleanly

The key factor with playing the short irons is, of course, accuracy and it is obvious that if you are ambitious to improve your game and reduce your score you can best do so by saving strokes on and around the green. The satisfaction of learning to drive well should not be at the expense of practising with the short irons. Accurate pitching with the Nos 8 and 9 irons, the wedge and sand wedge, call for standing a little nearer to the ball, and with the feet closer together. The ball should be positioned equidistant between the feet. Make sure the knees are flexed for balance, and concentrate on a three-quarter swing; but still be sure to make a full turn of the body, and hit through the ball. It is one thing to restrict the swing, quite another to quit on the shot. The art of successful short iron play is to hit the ball firmly and cleanly, taking the divot after it has been sent on its way. As ever, all the basic fundamentals of the golf swing, beginning with the need to keep the head steady throughout, still apply.

8

The Short Pitch and Chip Shots

The development of an effective short game – basically the ability to hole the ball in two shots from thirty yards or so off the green – is one of golf's easier challenges. Success can come rapidly with practice for the fundamentals involved are quite simple, and the rewards encourage dedication. The anguish of a poor drive or wayward iron approach is soon forgotten when the threat of a wasted stroke is overcome with a precisely judged chip or pitch and single putt. Better still is the feeling of 'getting down in two' for a birdie. Tournament professionals expect to do this as a matter of course, and there is no reason why the average amateur should not improve his scores by developing the technique and 'touch' required for a useful short game.

First, we need to be clear about the difference between the short pitch, usually played with the 9 iron, the wedge, or sand wedge, and the chip shot, best tackled with something like a No 7 iron. Different situations will dictate which method and club is wanted. The chip is generally regarded as a shot of low trajectory that causes the ball to roll a fair distance after landing on the green. But the short-game pitch is a high, floating shot, played with plenty of back-spin so that it 'bites', and the ball stops quickly on landing upon the green. Obviously, if a hazard of any kind, a bunker or a stream for example, stands between the ball and the green, then a pitch becomes necessary.

If however, a straightforward shot to the flag stick is offered, then the chip may well be the most suitable method.

The chip shot

The stance for the chip shot should be slightly open – the left foot withdrawn some six inches behind the right. By doing this, you will be partially facing the target and with the feet only six inches apart it helps to swing the club back slightly outside the line. The ball is positioned mid-way between the feet. Be sure to grip the club about three inches from the end of the shaft, what we call 'choking down' on the club. This will bring the ball closer to the body and sharpen the 'feel' that ultimately separates success and failure. The distance of the shot decides the length of the backswing, a half swing is usually enough – what we do not want at any cost is a long swing and deceleration on the way down in an attempt to soften the impact.

Fig. 56 The arms and clubshaft form a Y when the set-up is right for the chip shot.

Body movement must be restricted to an absolute minimum, the mental picture needed for the chip needs to be of a hands-and-arms swing. The object is to flight the ball onto the green, covering a third of the distance to the flag stick, and then to let it run the rest of the way. So a low, punched shot with restricted follow-through is demanded, and for this the wrists have to be kept fairly firm throughout the crisp, but smooth stroke. There is never a more important moment for keeping the head steady. The more delicate the shot the greater need there is for balance.

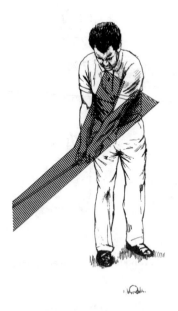

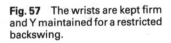

Fig. 57   The wrists are kept firm and Y maintained for a restricted backswing.

Fig. 58   Swing the Y as a one-piece unit through the ball.

The pitch

The short pitch calls for a successful combination of club and wrist action. The 52° loft of the wedge is usually sufficient and if not there is always the sand iron, 58°, though this rounded sole takes more practise to master. The basics are much the same as for the chip shot. Stand slightly open with the body turned towards the target, and address the ball off the middle of the stance. Pick the spot where you want the ball to land and imprint it on the mind for a clear mental picture. Instead of keeping the wrists firm as in the chip shot, put them to work. Let them punch the club face into the back of the ball with authority. It has to be a very definite 'hit down and through' shot every time. Do not scoop, have strong positive thoughts about extending the clubhead through the ball to waist height in the follow-through.

Fig. 59　Address position and three-quarter swing for short-iron accuracy.

Really, there is nothing very difficult about rolling 'three shots into two' as the tournament professionals call it. The key is not to be overwhelmed by the thought that only a short distance has to be covered – still hit the ball firmly.

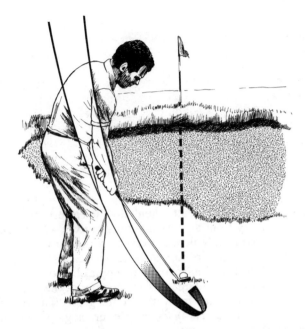

Fig. 60 To loft the ball high with a short pitch, open the stance and this will assist taking the club back outside the line.

9

Bunker Shots

One of the ironies of golf is that potentially the easiest shot in the game – the recovery from a *green-side sand bunker* – intimidates many players, and certainly all beginners, more than any other. Yet it is the only shot which in normal conditions actually calls for missing the ball. The basic, and extremely simple objective, is to use the club to 'explode' a small quantity of sand out of the bunker in such a way that it carries the ball with it to the green. The cardinal rule is to stay relaxed, but it is all too easy to turn negative thoughts into apprehension, and consequently tension. Certainly, the bunker shot needs to be respected, but never feared.

The overriding objective is, of course, to escape from the bunker at first attempt. There are few more demoralising experiences than taking two or more shots to recover from the sand. So, if the ball is positioned under the steep face of a bunker, making a forward shot in the general direction of the flag stick a risky business, then stop and think of a safer route. There is no shame in playing sideways to escape from a bunker.

As a general rule, never try to take the ball clean from the sand, i.e. you should not try to create a direct impact between clubface and ball as in a normal fairway iron shot. Use the club designed for the job, the sand wedge, and concentrate on having the ball fly out of the bunker on a cushion of sand. The normal green-side bunker shot requires an open clubface to strike the sand an inch or two behind the ball – the margin varies according to the distance of the shot to be hit – and to bounce through the sand at a depth of about an inch. In effect, this is like picking the sand up on a shovel, and hurling it forwards. The ball, sitting on top of the sand, will become part of the whole operation. So the mental image for this shot has to be of the ball taking a ride to the green on a 'divot' of sand.

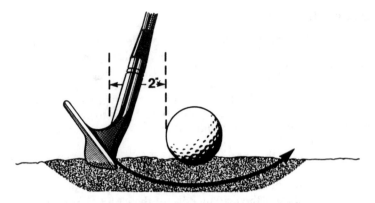

Fig. 61 The basic explosion shot with open clubface.

The preparations begin with the 'digging in' of your feet; the importance of this is to make sure that the base of the stance is an inch or so below the level of the ball. Then, with a normal swing, it becomes easy to have the clubhead ride under the ball. Do not forget that it is important to complete the follow-through, as this will help to keep your shot smooth and authoritative.

Fig. 62 Dig both feet down into the sand for a solid base at the right level, to enable the arc of the swing to be lower than the ball.

Attack the sand

Once the feet have been firmly embedded the ball should be addressed opposite the left heel with the stance open. The clubface must be held open throughout a natural out-to-in swing path. The apprehension felt by the average golfer towards bunker play leads all too often to a timid approach. More than anything, aggression is wanted. Maintain a smooth rhythm, but be sure to attack the sand. Keep body movement to a minimum, and make your hands and arms do the work.

Occasionally, this basic technique has to be varied to meet different circumstances. If the sand is exceptionally hard, or the ball is half buried, then use a closed face sand iron or even pitching wedge, in order for the leading edge of the club to knife under the ball. But still be sure to aim two inches behind as normal.

The cardinal rule governing *fairway bunker* shots is not to be greedy. Boldness must be tempered with caution. Care has to be taken in the selection of the right club. A perfectly struck shot which flies into the face of the bunker is not bad luck – it's bad thinking. Although you do want to hit your recovery shot the maximum distance, it is worth remembering that the primary objective when in a bunker is to get out at first attempt. The drill for recovering from a fairway bunker begins with wriggling the feet into the sand for a firm foundation. Address the ball from the centre of a square stance, and keep looking at the top of the ball as this encourages a clean strike. Grip firmly to guard against the clubface being turned off line, and concentrate on an active leg action. Above all, think positively, accept that becoming a good bunker player is only a matter of practice. There is absolutely no need to be intimidated by sand.

Fig. 63 Remember:
– ball opposite left heel
– open stance and body
– 60% of weight on left leg
– open clubface throughout the swing
– aim 2 inches behind the ball

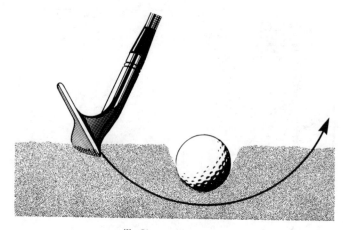

(i) Close the clubface and use a full-power swing to dig the ball out of a buried lie.

(ii) Use a pitching wedge or closed-face sand iron for a very deeply buried lie, as the sharper edge knifes into the sand.

Fig. 64   Bad lies in bunkers

(iii) Use a strong, down-ward, chopping blow to escape from the 'fried egg' lie.

Fig. 65   Dig the feet well into the sand, and use shut clubface, for dealing with a ball buried in a bunker.

10

The Art of Putting

If there is such a thing as a short cut to lower scores in golf then it is by the putting route. Only one statistic is needed to explain why. The putter is far and away the most used club in the bag – thirty-six times on average for the regulation 18 holes. Therefore, it must offer the greatest opportunity for saving shots through improvement. Tournament professionals recognise this fact by practising their putting for many more hours than any other department of the game. Consequently, the best among them will average 28 to 30 putts a round over an entire season.

Consistently good putting depends upon confidence, and this in turn requires the development of two, equally important, basic skills. A reliable, habitual or 'repeating' stroke that works under pressure is wanted, along with the ability to 'read' the contours and the speed of different greens. Putting has long been accepted as a game within a game, and there are literally hundreds of conflicting methods. Occasionally, the beginner will discover a natural instinct that will make him the envy of far more accomplished golfers. More likely however, you will need to school yourself in the fundamentals of putting, and then use these as the foundation on which to experiment and decide which slight variations best suit. Even then you will soon learn that what works one day can bring nothing but disappointment the next, and there will be no end to the process of experimentation. For inside golf, putting is a law unto itself. There is no one way to putt well, and a day of watching the tournament professionals gives ample proof of this fact. They all have their different styles, and they will always be seen crowding the practice green, testing more and more variations in a never-ending search for improvement.

However fickle putting may be, the fundamentals involved remain firm. The first requirement is to start building confidence by adopting a grip that is comfortable. Most good putters favour what we call the *reverse overlap* – the same principle of thumbs down the shaft, the back of the left hand and the palm of the right hand facing the target, but with the left index finger this time riding over the little finger of the right hand. To putt well, the hands have to work as a unit, and with a delicate sense of 'feel'. The reverse overlap is recommended to the beginner because it is most likely to meet both needs, but that is not to say that other methods are without merit. Extreme variations, such as holding the putter with the hands separated and the left below the right, have been known to win championships. It is all a matter of personal preference. What works for you has to be the best.

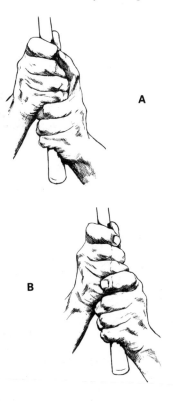

Fig. 66 Two variations of the 'reverse overlap'. Putting grip **A** is the most popular.

There can be no argument however about the absolute necessity to keep tension out of the putting stroke. Otherwise the door is opened to creating the dreaded 'yips' – uncontrolled stabbing at the ball instead of a smooth strike and this is usually an extremely difficult affliction to cure. Prevention is much simpler.

To begin, stand to the ball in a completely comfortable manner. The slightest degree of strain is guaranteed to wreck a good putting stroke. Let your arms hang loosely, grip the club firmly but still leaving a light sensitive touch in your fingers, and position your head directly over the ball which is addressed off the inside of the left heel. Your feet and the hips should be slightly open at the address.

Fig. 67   Hold the head steady, directly above the ball.

Now we have established a set-up that allows a mental picture of swinging the putter like a pendulum. This is done by ensuring that the shoulders, arms and hands work as a single component. The object is to form them into a perfect triangle which will rock backwards and forwards.

Fig. 68   The 'rocking triangle' principle for putting: slightly open stance . . . head steady . . .

It was fashionable in the past to have the hands dominate the stroke, and there were players who enjoyed tremendous success with a wristy method. The 'triangle' influence is now dominant in the modern game. The 'feel' in the hands is rarely the same two days in succession, and so making them the all-governing factor is likely to encourage an inconsistent putting stroke. The responsibility is too much for the hands alone. The answer is to let the 'triangle' formation of the arms and shoulders do the work together. They need a solid base on which to operate, and this is best achieved with the feet about nine inches apart, the knees flexed forwards and inwards, the weight evenly distributed, and the body held still throughout the stroke. Keep the clubhead as low as possible on the backswing and low again on the follow-through after a firm, positive, striking of the ball. Concentrate on maintaining the triangle and making a good strike.

Fig. 69 ... hit through the ball ... be positive ...

Fig. 70 ... same length for follow-through as for backswing.

Always adopt a positive, even an aggressive attitude; this will help you to hole many more putts than those who are so timid that they constantly leave the ball short of the hole. There is nothing like making a bold putt for building up confidence, and there is nothing like confidence for helping you to do it again. So much to do with the art of putting is in the mind – shun negative tactics like the plague.

The development of a sound and repeating putting stroke is no good, however, without the ability to 'read' a green. The art of reading the pace of a green does not come easily. Indeed, the very best of tournament professionals can on occasions, more especially early in a round as they adjust to conditions, be seen committing an error of judgement by putting the ball well past the hole – 'being strong' – or leaving it short, known as 'being weak'. Rarely however, do they repeat the same mistake. They quickly learn from every lapse, and it is equally important for you to do so as a means of improving. The terms 'fast' and 'slow' greens have obvious definitions. Championship and major tournament venues generally favour, weather and other circumstances permitting, the preparation of fast greens which encourage a smooth, swift rolling of the ball from a delicate use of the putter. The faster the green, within reason, the sterner the examination of a player's skills, and not just with the putter. A fast green places a high premium on the accuracy of approach shots. There is always a 'right' and a 'wrong' spot to place the ball. Twenty feet above the hole, creating the daunting prospect of the first putt sending the ball sliding past the hole to keep rolling downhill as far again, is definitely the 'wrong' place. Top golfers are always careful to reduce the threat of fast greens by hitting their approach shots as close as possible below the hole, so leaving an uphill putt and the chance to attack. Many factors are involved in the preparation of fast greens: weather, soil, drainage, fine grasses, and, always the expertise of the greenkeeper with his mower blades set far lower than your lawn at home could withstand. Seaside courses, helped by sandy soil and drying winds, are best suited to really fast greens. In contrast, parkland courses where the soil can be heavy and the grasses require considerable watering, generally have slower greens which demand a much bolder putting stroke. The tendency then is to leave putts short of the hole.

The degree to which a green is fast or slow is mostly a matter of 'feel' for the golfer. But there are ways that you can help yourself. Always learn from an opponent or partner who putts first. Also, drill yourself into the habit of always spending a few minutes on the practice putting green before going to the first tee. There is nothing more damaging to your confidence than the experience of taking three putts at the opening hole after being surprised by the pace of the green. It can help on fast greens to use a light blade putter for a more delicate touch. Or, if the greens are extremely lush and slow, try a putter with a heavy head. Remember, every problem in golf has an answer.

11

Trouble Shots

The enjoyment of playing golf is dependent upon acceptance of the axiom that to err is only human; the perfect golfer will always be a figment of the imagination. Even Open champions rarely claim the satisfaction of hitting more than five or six shots of 100 per cent quality in a single round. Trouble, and escaping from it, is very much an integral part of the game for players of all standards. So learning to cope with the inevitable problems of golf is an essential part of your basic golfing education. The difference between good and bad golfers is never more marked than when they are confronted with trouble.

Beginners frequently share a compulsive urge to attack their problem as quickly as possible. Do not be obsessed with the need to 'get it over with', as this leads to an unthinking assault upon the ball. The result, often as not, is the replacing of one problem with another. Try instead to approach trouble in quite the opposite manner: always take time to study a dilemma on the course with the concentration of a chess player deciding on his next complicated move. Let the rule, *Think it out*, govern your approach, as there is always more than one solution to a problem, and haste certainly does not allow them all to be carefully considered. Remember, too, that there is no law in golf which compels the ball to be hit forward. Sometimes, hitting the ball to the side, or even away from the hole, offers the best escape route from a worrying situation. You should never be too proud to cut your losses in this way. Always play within your own limits; do not press on regardless and hope for a miracle.

When faced with trouble, 80 per cent of the solution lies in the mind. When the situation is desperately serious, do not overlook, as so many beginners do, the simplest solution of all – take advantage of the rules of golf, pick the ball up, and carry it to the best point of safety allowed at the cost of one penalty shot. This can be a lot less expensive than thrashing away wildly in the trees. 'Trouble' shots are an everyday part of golf, and the technique needed to success-fully meet their challenge can be mastered with practice.

Uphill lie (Figure 71)

As with all shots that do not allow a level stance, maintaining a proper *balance* throughout the swing is a problem when faced with an uphill lie. Take care to stand perpendicular to the slope, address the ball closer to the left foot than usual, and – because it is obviously going to fly high – take a club one grade stronger than you would normally use for the distance to be covered (a 5 iron instead of a 6, for example).

The gradient will add more weight to the *right* side of the body, making it more difficult to keep clear of the *left* side of the body in the downswing. This will encourage the hands to become more active, and so there will be a tendency to hit the ball to the left. So begin compensating at the address position by aiming a little right of the target.

Downhill lie (Figure 72)

Any problem shot puts an added importance on maintaining a good *rhythm*, so be sure to swing smoothly. Address the ball more towards the right foot, pick the clubhead up a little more quickly with earlier wrist action to counteract the slope, and concentrate on a really solid *down-and-through* impact following the contour of the slope for as long as possible. Guard against swaying and falling forward in the shot, and this time aim off a shade to the left. The natural tendency will be to hit the ball with a *fade* or left-to-right flight. Obviously, the trajectory of the ball is going to be lower. This makes a club with more loft advisable, a 7 iron instead of a 6 iron, for example, according to the distance of the shot.

Fig. 71 The uphill lie encourages the ball to fly left.

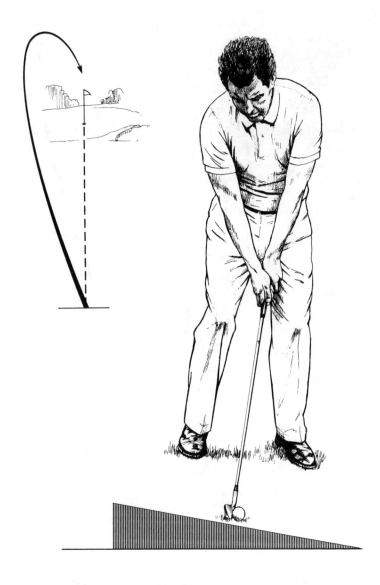

Fig. 72   Allow for a fade or slice from a downhill lie.

Side hill lie – ball below feet

The left to right flight of a slice now becomes the danger, because of the need to stand closer to the ball and adopt an *upright* swing. Aim slightly left, therefore; flex the knees more than usual, keep the weight on the heels, address the ball towards the left foot, grip the club at full length, keep the head steady to help balance, and play the shot with hands and arms.

Side hill lie – ball above feet

Take a slightly shorter grip of the club – choke down two or three centimetres – to compensate for the flatter swing this situation compels. Keep the weight on the front of the feet to offset the tendency to fall back off balance during the swing. The need to stand further away from the ball, and swing more round the body creates the danger of a right to left shot. Allow for this by aiming to the right of the target.

Fig. 73 **A** When played from below the feet, the ball tends to take a left-to-right flight.

B From above the feet, the ball will tend to hook.

Ball buried in bunker

First, forget heroics, and settle for just getting it safely out of the hazard. Turn the toe of the sand wedge in slightly to *close the clubface* at address, and this will ensure that the leading edge, rather than the flange, will first make contact with the sand at impact. The object is to 'knife' *under the ball and through the sand.* Address the ball towards the right foot and hit down sharply. Go *right through* with the shot: whatever you do, do not become a victim of the most common of all bunker play faults by quitting at impact. Lead with the hands, and put plenty of energy to work.

Fig. 74 When the ball buried, close the clubface and use the leading edge like a knife, to hit down, under and through with plenty of aggression. The follow-through is important.

Intentional slice

Trees and other obstacles have a nasty habit of blocking the golfer's target line. So learning to 'bend' a ball, as opposed to hitting it straight, can prove extremely helpful on occasions. When the ball has to be hit on a left to right path, then a fade, or more pronounced slice, is wanted. Firstly, remember that it is the *open set up*, and the *outside-to-in swing path* with an open clubface, that produces the intentional slice. Pick a spot left of the target as the point of aim, and address the ball towards the front of a narrow, open stance.

Fig. 75 An intentional slice can get you out of trouble.

Use the normal grip but with the clubface 'open' or, more precisely, lofted. Select a stronger club than normal, because both the 'bending' of the ball and the need for a restricted three-quarter swing will cause loss of distance. Contrary to everything that has been said before, in this shot the clubhead has to be taken outside the target line on the backswing. Then the outside-to-in path of the downswing will cause the clubface to cut across the ball at impact. The faster the hand action, the more the side-spin imparted on the ball. You will not master this shot without considerable practice, so do not be too ambitious.

 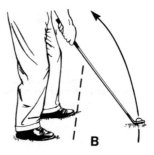

Fig. 76 **A** Open stance for slice. **B** Closed stance for hook.

Intentional hook

Drop down a club or two – a 6 or 7 iron instead of a 5 – for this shot because a hook causes the ball to run further. Again, use the normal grip, but with the clubface 'closed' or, more precisely, 'de-lofted'. Also, close the stance by pulling the right foot back behind the left, aim right of the target, and concentrate on swinging on an *inside-to-out* path with closed clubface. Whip the hands through the shot, let them roll over, and watch the ball fly from right to left.

Fig. 77 Use a more lofted club for the intentional hook, and allow the hands to roll over.

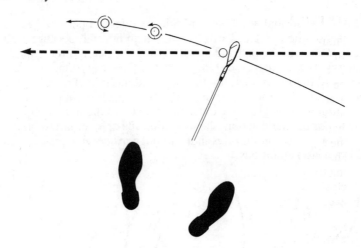

Fig. 78 To hook – close stance, aim right of the target, and whip the hands through the shot with an in-to-out swing.

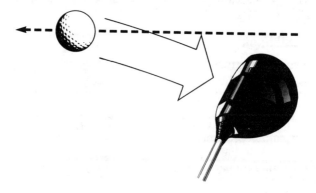

Fig. 79 **A** Use the normal grip for an intentional hook, close or de-loft the clubface, and remember that the right-to-left flight of the ball will cause it to run further.

B Take the club back inside the line to hook.

Heavy rough

The main danger here is an excess of ambition. Accept that the primary objective has to be getting the ball back into play with one shot. So settle for the club that will do the job with the greatest degree of safety. Play the ball off the middle of the stance, choke down on the club to encourage a *compact swing*, pick the club up sharply and hit *down and through* with a slightly open face. Remember that there will be a strong cushion of grass between the clubface and the ball at impact, so backspin will be minimal, if there is any at all. The more likely result is a low trajectory 'flyer' with overspin, causing the ball to run further than usual. This cushion of grass will also close the clubface at impact so take care to address the ball with the face slightly open, pointing to the right of the target.

Barefaced lies

Golfers have to become accustomed to the misfortune of having good shots finish with the ball lying on bare patches of fairway, on paths, or in old divot marks. One of golf's older adages is 'it was never meant to be a fair game anyway'.

Fig. 80 Let the hands lead the clubhead for a low, running shot. Use a three-quarter swing with a stronger club than normal. Restrict the follow-through for a low or punched shot.

The object is to stay calm, not to become tense, and to know how to deal with the situation. The answer is to take a straighter-faced club than you normally would for the distance, settle for a *three-quarter* swing, and *punch* the shot from the *back* of the stance. There will be a real danger of the clubface being turned at impact, so *grip firmly*.

Fig. 81 Grip firmly to prevent the clubhead turning, and punch the ball from the back of the stance, to escape from a divot.

A

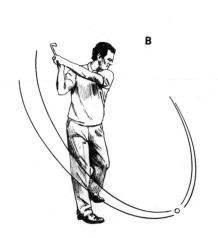

B

C

Fig. 82

A Normal swing plane. **B** Flat swing encourages hook.

C Upright out-to-in swing encourages slice.

12

Diagnosing Common Faults

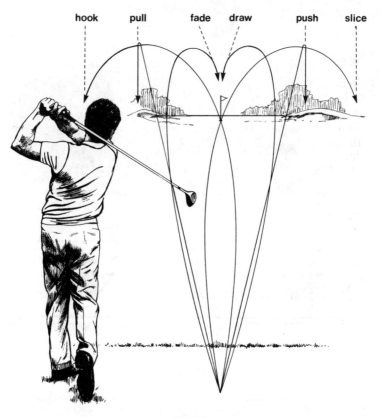

Fig. 83

The golfer has yet to be born who does not occasionally send the ball soaring away with the destructive left-to-right flight of an unwanted slice. What causes this most common and costly of all faults, and what is the cure? If only it were as simple as that. A slice can result from any one of a dozen set-up and swing malfunctions. Consequently, there are just as many possible solutions. Often, to complicate matters even further, a combination of two or more causes has to be untangled. And the same applies to all other faults that you must expect to encounter during your development as a golfer. A primary checklist, that can be useful on the practice ground for the purpose of self-analysis, is given below. However, if the problem persists, then you should seek the help of a professional teacher before it becomes ingrained in the swing as a habit.

The slice

Effect: a 'pure slice' starts the ball left of the target, then the side spin imparted by an open clubface and outside-to-in swing path causes it to curve to the right.

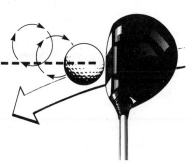

Fig. 84 The clubhead path in a slice.

Causes

A   Weak grip, the hands turned too far left, causing only one knuckle of the left hand to show.

B   Addressing the ball with an open clubface, or pronating the wrists to open it during the takeaway.

C   Faulty set-up with the ball positioned too far forward causing the hips and shoulders to aim left of the target so that the club will go outside the target line on the backswing.

D   Failure to complete the pivot; and starting the downswing with the shoulders instead of a lateral hip movement, i.e. failing to use the legs during the swing.

Fig. 85   The slice.

The hook

Effect: side-spin caused by a closed clubface and inside-to-out swing path giving the right-to-left flight of a hooked shot.

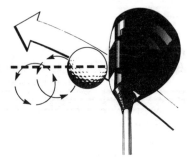

Fig. 86   The clubhead path in a hook.

Causes

A Strong grip with the hands too much to the right, four knuckles of the left hand showing.

B Addressing the ball with a closed clubface, or hooding it on the takeaway.

C Faulty set-up with ball too far back, causing hips and shoulders to aim to the right of the target, creating an excessive in-to-out swing.

D Failure to turn hips and transfer weight to the left side for impact.

Fig. 87 The hook.

The pull

Effect: the ball flies on a straight line left of the target.

Causes
A The set-up wrongly aimed to the left, with the ball too far forward at the address position.
B Holding the clubface square to an outside-to-in swing path.
C Poor balance, falling back on the right foot during the down-swing.

The push

Effect: the ball is hit straight, but to the right of the target.

Causes
A Set up aimed to the right.
B Ball too far back in the stance.
C Going outside the line on the backswing, then looping on the way down to compensate.
D Failing to clear the hips at impact.

The shank

Effect: the *shank* or *socket* occurs when the ball is struck with the *hosel* rather than the clubface, causing it to fly right at 45°.

Causes
A Standing too close to the ball and swaying forwards on to the toes during the down-swing.
B Flat swing, and rolling the clubface open.
C Lazy hand action.

Fig. 88 The shank.

The top

Effect: when the ball is *topped* it means that it has been hit high on its perimeter, instead of solidly in the back, causing the ball to travel little or no distance, low to the ground.

Causes

A Angle of attack on ball too steep.

B Too much body action on downswing.

C Swinging too quickly.

D Standing too close to the ball at address.

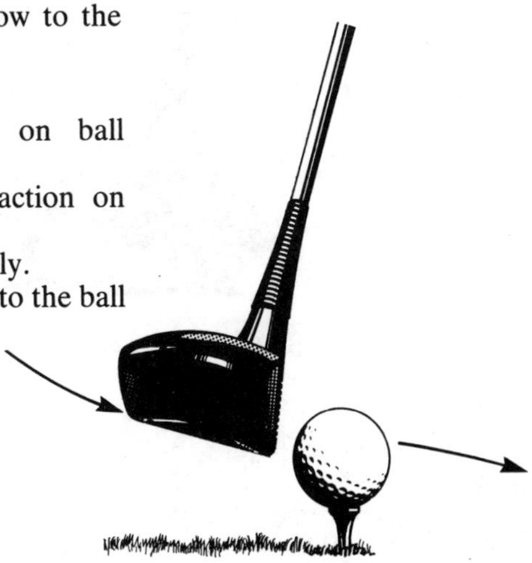

Fig. 89 The topped shot: the bottom half of the clubface strikes the top half of the ball.

Skying

Effect: the opposite of topping (although the causes are similar): the ball soars up into the air and consequently loses considerable distance.

Causes

A Poor set-up, encouraging bending of the wrists and lifting of the clubhead too early in the backswing.

B Failure to transfer the weight back to the left foot on the downswing.

C Angle of attack on the ball is too steep, leading to a chopping action which results in contact being made with the top of the clubhead instead of the middle of the clubface.

D Tilting the shoulders instead of turning on a flat plane.

Fig. 90   Skying the drive.

The fluff

Effect: More often known as 'hitting fat' (or 'hitting thick'), this shot results from the clubhead making contact with the ground before the ball. This will usually turn the clubface away from square, and the ball can fly in any direction.

Causes
A   Angle of attack too flat.
B   Hitting too early.
C   Not turning the hips out of the way on the downswing.
D   Bad posture at address.

Inconsistency

Effect: the worst fault of all, for it means a succession of different mistakes, causing extreme frustration.

Causes
A   Bad posture, leading to a poor sense of balance.
B   Swinging too quickly.
C   Failing to take time to develop a mental picture of what is needed to make the shot a success.

Glossary of Golfing Terms

ace   Hole in one, a feat with odds of 40,000–1 against for the average golfer.
address   Positioning of the body and club in readiness to play a shot.
air shot   To swing and miss the ball.
albatross   Score of three under par on one hole, i.e. to hole in one at a par four or in two shots at a par five.
all square   State of tied match.
approach shot   Any stroke played with the intention of putting the ball on the green.
apron   Mown area immediately surrounding green.
arc   Path taken by clubhead throughout swing.
assistant   Trainee professional golfer.
away   The ball farthest from the hole is said to be away.

back holes   Second half of the course, i.e. last nine holes.
back marker   Player with the lowest handicap in the group.
backspin   Clockwise spinning action imparted on the ball by the lofted and grooved face of a club to help control its flight and roll.
backswing   Movement of body and club from address position to top of the swing.
back tee   Slang for championship tee.
baffy   Obsolete wooden club equivalent to No 4 wood.
ball   American-sized ball of 42.67 mm (1.68 inches) is in the process of completely replacing the British ball of 41.15 mm (1.62 inches) diameter. Both weigh 45.92 grams (1.62 ounces).
ball marker   Plastic disc or small coin used to mark precise position of ball on green before lifting to clean.
better ball match   A match in which two partners form a team and only the better score of either player counts at each hole.
birdie   Score of one below par.
bisque   Handicap stroke that can be claimed at any hole during a match.
blade   Striking area of iron club.
blading   Term for a topped shot that causes the ball to fly low or run along the ground.

blaster   Slang name for a wedge.

blind shot   Hitting to a target hidden by rising ground, trees or other course feature.

bogey   First introduced as the score a first class amateur should make at each hole. Now universally recognised as denoting a score of one shot more than par, e.g. taking five strokes at a par four hole. Six shots would be a *double bogey*.

borrow   Aiming to one side of the hole by varying amounts to allow for the contours of a green when putting – 'Borrow two feet to the left.' Also known as break.

brassey/brassie   Name for a No 2 wood club which has fallen out of fashion.

break   See *Borrow*

bulger   Driver with convex face.

bunker   Depression in the ground filled with sand – an intended and maintained hazard.

buggy   Colloquial term for motorised golf cart.

bye   Secondary and informal match played over holes remaining to the 18th when the main game is completed.

caddie   Person engaged to carry player's clubs and offer advice when asked.

caddie cart   Two-wheeled trolley for carrying clubs.

callaway   Handicapping system in which a player's score is determined by his worst holes.

card   Official score card of the course.

carry   Distance from where ball is hit and where it lands.

casual water   Temporary accumalation of water, snow or ice on the course, not forming any part of a declared water hazard, and from which a player is allowed to lift the ball clear without penalty.

centre shaft   Club with shaft fitted to centre of head.

chip   Short, low, running shot.

choke   Slang term for losing one's nerve.

choke down   Hold the club with hands lower than usual on the grip for short, delicate shots, or to reduce the distance potential of a full shot.

cleat   Metal stud for golf shoes.

cleek   Old iron club equivalent to No 2 iron.

closed clubface   Club aimed left of target at address.

closed stance   Player's body is aimed right of target with right foot drawn back behind left at address position.

clubface   Lofted and grooved area of clubhead with which ball is hit.

concede   Term of surrender – putt, hole or match.

course   Ground within clearly defined boundaries on which game is played.

cup   Colloquial term for the hole.

cut   See *Slice*

cut-up shot   Sidespin deliberately imparted to give the ball a curving flight from left to right.

dead   See *Gimme*

dimples   Indentations – averaging 330 – on the cover of a golf ball designed to maximise its aerodynamic qualities.

divot   Turf cut from under ball in the playing of an iron shot.

dog-leg   Hole designed with angled fairway.

dog licence   Slang for 7/6 result in match play contest – derived from seven shillings and sixpence once being the cost of a dog licence.

dormey/dormie   Situation in match play when a player cannot be beaten because he leads by the same number of holes as there are still left to play.

driving range   Area specifically designed and maintained for practice.

downswing   Movement of body and club from top of swing to point of impact.

draw shot   Controlled right-to-left curving flight.

driver   Club designed with minimum loft to give tee shots maximum distance.

drive the green   Hit a tee shot that reaches the green.

duck hook   Shot that curves sharply to the left of target line.

eagle   Score of two shots under par at one hole, e.g. three at a par five.

eclectic   Best score at each hole on one course over a number of rounds.

equity   Method of resolving disputes not convered by rules.

etiquette   The code of good manners, sportsmanship and respect for other players on the course that upholds the tradition of golf being a game for gentlemen.

explosion shot   Recovery stroke from bunker which calls for hitting the sand rather than ball.

fade   Controlled left-to-right flight.

fairway   Mown grass between tee and green.

fat shot   Hitting ground behind ball instead of making clean contact.

featherie/feathery   Ball, which replaced the original wooden ball, with a leather cover stuffed tight with feathers, used until about 1848, and now a valuable collectors' item.

flagstick   Pole of six feet or more in height, bearing flag, which signifies position of hole on each green.

flange   Ridge along base of iron club or putter.

flat swing   Act of swinging the club on a plane nearer to being horizontal than vertical.

flier   Shot lacking backspin to control flight and roll – usually the result of playing from rough where the thick grass forms a cushion between clubface and ball at impact.

fluff   A bad mishit.

follow-through   Continuation of the swing after impact.

fore   Warning cry of 'Fore' is shouted by golfer to alert others in danger of being hit by ball.

forward press   Slight movement of the hands – not the clubhead – at the address position to guard against tension.

fourball   Match involving four players, each playing his own game, though two may form a partnership for a *better ball* score.

foursomes   Two players in partnership hit alternate shots with one ball.

fried egg lie   Ball half buried in bunker.

gimme   Putt so short that it is considered unmissable and worthy of being conceded in match play golf. In stroke play or medal golf all putts have to be holed. Gimme putts are also known as *dead*.

grain   See *Nap*

grand slam   First used to describe the 1930 unique achievement of Bobby Jones winning the Open and Amateur Championships of Britain and the United States. Now updated to mean the Open Championship conducted by the Royal and Ancient Golf Club of St. Andrews; and the US Masters, Open and PGA Championships.

green   Those areas of a course specifically prepared for putting. Also the original name for a course, that form surviving in the terms green fee, green committee.

greensome   Informal format which calls for both players forming a partnership to drive and then select the better-placed ball to continue playing the hole by hitting alternate shots in foursomes fashion.

grip   Method of holding a club or the 'handle' of a club.

ground under repair   Areas of course officially marked as unfit for play and from which a golfer is entitled to move his ball without penalty.

guttie/gutty   Solid Golf ball made of gutta-percha, a rubbery substance, which replaced the *feathery* and was in use until the early 1900s.

half   Opponents have 'halved' when they complete a hole in the same number of shots or finish a match tied.

handicap   Official allowance of shots based on a golfer's average performance against the scratch score of a course, a system that allows players of all standards to compete with each other on equal terms.

hanging lie   Shot that has to be played off sloping ground.

haskell   Forerunner of the modern golf ball, rubber-cored, introduced early 1900s to replace the gutty named after the American Coburn Haskell who invented a machine to wind rubber thread under tension around a central core.

hazards   Bunkers or any intended areas of water on the course.

head   The striking part of a club.

heel   Angle formed by neck and face of a club.

hickory   Type of wood used to make golf club shafts before steel shafts were legalised in 1929 (1924 in USA).

hitting early   Starting to uncock the wrists too soon in the downswing.

hitting late   Delaying the uncocking of the wrists in an attempt to increase clubhead acceleration and therefore hit the ball a greater distance.

hole Rules decree that it must be 4¼ inches (108 mm) in diameter and at least 4 inches (100 mm) deep.

hole in one Hitting tee shot into the hole.

home of golf Tradition reference to St Andrews, in Scotland.

honour The right to play first from the tee – a matter of agreement at the start of a match but thereafter the honour automatically goes to the player who did best at the previous hole. In the event of a hole being halved then the player who held the honour retains it.

hooding Rotating the face of the club towards the target, thereby reducing the normal loft.

hook Shot with sidespin that causes pronounced right-to-left flight.

hosel Neck or socket in which the shaft joins the clubhead.

impact Precise point at which clubface strikes ball.

in play A ball is 'in play' from the moment it has been struck on the tee until it comes to rest in the hole.

irons Clubs with metal heads and faces with lofts varied in sequence to determine trajectory and distance of shots.

jigger Utility club once popular for playing chip shots.

jungle Slang for trees, bushes, heavy rough or any punishing form of natural growth bordering fairways.

lag Long putt played cautiously with intention of leaving the ball close to the hole (as opposed to a bold, attacking stroke in an attempt to hole out at the risk of running past the hole if unsuccessful).

lie Situation of the ball at rest – a *good lie* if 'sitting up' well on the fairway; a *bare (barefaced) lie* if on a pathway or some other worn surface; a *bad lie* if in thick grass, a divot or similar trouble. Also describes angle between shaft and clubhead.

line Direction in which a shot needs to be hit.

links Golf course built on sandy, seaside terrain.

lip Edge or rim of the hole – a ball which hits the hole but fails to fall in is said to have 'lipped' out.

local knowledge Advantage enjoyed by a player competing on a course he knows well.

local rules Additional rules to meet specific circumstances at every course.

loft Angle of the clubface.

loose impediments Natural objects – stones, leaves, litter etc – that player is allowed to remove when they hamper his ability to hit the ball.

lost ball A ball is officially lost if it cannot be found within five minutes.

marker Person designated to keep score.

mashie Old iron club equivalent to No 5 iron.

match play Contest decided on the winning of individual holes.

medal play Contest decided on the total number of strokes taken to complete the course, more correctly called stroke-play.

mixed foursome   Partnership of one man and one woman hitting alternate shots with one ball.

municipal course   Operated by the local authority for the general public – as opposed to private club – and an ideal starting point for newcomers to golf.

mulligan   Allowing a player starting a game to hit a second drive if he is dissatisfied with his first. Not condoned by the rules.

muscle memory   Automatic observance of correct swing movements developed by disciplined and repetitive practice.

nap   Tendency of grass to grow at an angle and influence the roll of the ball on greens. Also known as grain.

nassau   Dividing one round of golf into three separate matches for betting purposes – first nine holes, back nine, and over-all 18.

never up, never in   Term of condemnation for putting short of hole.

niblick   Old club equivalent to No 8 iron.

nineteenth   First extra hole to decide tied match or, more generally, colloquial expression for clubhouse bar.

obstructions   Man made objects from which the golfer is entitled to relief.

open stance   Left foot drawn back so that player's body is turned slightly towards target at position of address.

out of bounds   All areas outside the defined limits of the course.

outside agency   Any agency, person or animal, not competitively involved in a match, e.g. referee, observer, steward – but liable to accidentally obstruct or move ball.

par   Indicates score a scratch handicap golfer is expected to make at a hole – i.e. holes up to 250 yards (228 metres) in length are rated as par 3s; between 251 yards and 475 yards (434 metres) inclusive as par 4s; and anything longer as par 5.

penalty stroke   Added to score for taking relief under the rules or infringing rules.

persimmon   Hardwood specially favoured for the making of club heads.

PGA   Professional Golfers Association.

pick and drop   Act of picking ball up and dropping it in another spot as allowed by the rules in specified circumstances, e.g. taking relief from casual water and unplayable lie.

pin   Slang term for flagstick.

pin high   Ball that comes to rest level with the flagstick, either on or off the green.

pitch   Short, high shot. Hence, pitching wedge.

pitch mark   Indentation made by ball hitting ground. Eitiquette demands that a player always repair his pitch mark on a green.

pivot   Turning of body in the backswing.

plane   Angle at which the club is swung, in relation to the ground.

play off   Extra hole or holes played to settle a tie.

plugged   Said of ball embedded in its own pitch mark.

preferred lie   Right to improve lie of the ball under temporary local rule intended to offset abnormal ground conditions.

press   The fault of trying to hit the ball too hard; also a form of gambling – generally accepted as claiming the right to strike an extra wager on going two down in a match.

provisional ball   Playing second ball to save time when suspecting that first might be lost or out of bounds.

pull   Ball flying straight left of target.

punch   Shot played with short backswing and hands ahead of ball at impact to keep ball on low trajectory.

push   Ball flying straight right of target.

putt   Shot made with a putter on a green.

putter   Straight-faced club designed for use on greens.

quail high shot   Extremely low-flying shot.

quit on shot   Failure to continue the swing after impact.

rabbit   Novice player.

rap   Deliberate putting style which calls for short, decisive stroke and stopping blade of putter at impact.

recovery shot   Hitting ball to safety from position of trouble.

regulation   Number of shots appropriate to a hole by a good golfer.

relief   To take relief is to pick up the ball and drop it in another spot as allowed by the rules in specified (unplayable) circumstances.

rough   Long grass cultivated to punish shots which miss the fairways or greens.

round robin   Match play competition in which every competitor plays all the others, the one achieving most victories being the overall winner.

Royal and Ancient   The Royal and Ancient Golf Club of St Andrews, the governing body of the game throughout most of the world.

rub of the green   Golfing luck, good or bad, created by an eccentric bounce or outside agency influencing the outcome of a shot and for which there is no provision under the rules.

run   Distance a ball travels after it pitches.

run up shot   Low shot into the green with the intention of having the ball roll to the hole as opposed to a lofted pitch.

Ryder Cup   Biennial team match between players from the PGA European Tour and the United States PGA Tour.

sand iron   Club with broad, rounded sole and extremely lofted face, specifically designed for bunker shots.

scratch   A scratch golfer is one with zero handicap.

senior   Professional golfers are officially recognised as seniors (or *veterans*) for tournament purposes on reaching the age of 50, and amateurs at 55.

single   Match between two players.

shank   Shot when contact is made with the neck of the club, causing the ball to fly off at an eccentric angle. Also known as a socket.

sky   To hit an exceptionally high but short shot.

slice   Shot that sends ball flying in a pronounced left-to-right curve. Also known as a cut.

socket   See *shank*

sole   Base of club head.

split hand   Putting method with hands kept apart to grip club.

spoon   Old wooden club equivalent to No 3 wood.

square stance   Both feet are parallel to the target line at the address position.

Stableford   Competition format based on points – one point at every hole the player scores a nett one-over-par bogey; two points for a par; three points for a birdie; four points for an eagle; five points for an albatross. Invented by Dr Frank Stableford, member of the Royal Liverpool and Wallasey Clubs, in 1931.

stance   The act of a player placing his feet in position in readiness to hit the ball.

standard scratch score   Every course has an SSS rating based on length and difficulty, and this becomes the score a scratch golfer is expected to make in fair weather.

stroke   The act of intentionally hitting the ball.

stroke hole   Where a player receives or gives a stroke to his opponents under the handicapping system.

stroke index   Chart detailing stroke holes in order of priority.

stroke play   Also known as medal play, or card-and-pencil golf. An examination of how many shots a player needs to complete the course.

sudden death   Play-off to decide a tie.

swingweight   Ratio of weight, length and balance intended to ensure that all clubs in a set are perfectly matched.

takeaway   Start of the backswing.

tee   Prepared area from which golfer begins to play every hole.

tee marker   Usually a box, cone or plaque indicating exactly where on the tee the drive must be hit.

tee peg   Wooden or plastic aid on which ball can be perched for tee shots only.

tempo   The rhythm vital to a good swing.

texas wedge   American expression applied to a putter when used off the green for an approach shot.

threeball   Three players forming a match.

through the green   All of the course except teeing grounds, greens and hazards.

tiger   Golfer of high ability.

topping   Hitting top half of the ball so that it scuttles along the ground.

topspin   All called overspin, opposite of backspin, intended to make the ball run a maximum distance.

tradesman's entrance Back or side edge of the hole.

trolley Caddie cart for carrying clubs.

trap Slang: bunkers are known as traps on American courses.

turn Position reached after nine holes.

upright swing Act of swinging club more towards the vertical than horizontal.

valley of sin Famous hollow in front of the 18th green on the Old Course at St Andrews, in Scotland.

Vardon grip Method of holding club popularised by Harry Vardon, winner of the Open Championship six times between 1896 and 1914.

velocity Manufacture of golf balls is governed by a velocity rule with a limit of 250 feet (76.2 metres) per second.

veteran see *senior*

waggle Movement of hands and clubhead at address position to release tension while establishing sense of 'feel' and rhythm.

Walker Cup Biennial amateur team match between Britain and Ireland, and the United States.

water hazard Any sea, lake, pond, river, ditch, surface drainage ditch or other open water course whether or not containing water, and anything of a similar nature.

wedge Broad-sole, lofted club used for short, high pitches and a variety of trouble shots.

whipping Twine or filament binding to secure heads of wooden clubs.

winter rules Temporary concessions – such as allowing the ball to be picked up and cleaned on the fairways – to make play possible and protect the course against undue wear in abnormal conditions.

wry neck Club with curved neck.

yardage chart Personal measurements, listing landmarks on each hole of a course to help a player judge the distance of any shot.

yips A nervous affliction which makes controlling the hands difficult, especially when putting. Also known as the twitch.

Rules of Golf

as approved by the
Royal and Ancient Golf Club
of St. Andrews, Scotland

and the
United States Golf Association

26th Edition Effective 1 January 1988

The Royal and Ancient Golf Club of St. Andrews and the United States Golf Association have carried out their customary quadrennial review of the Rules of Golf and have agreed upon certain amendments which they believe will improve the Rules.

The extensive changes in the Rules which were introduced in 1984 have received universal approval. Consequently, a minimal number of substantive changes were considered necessary. These are summarised on pages 103–4.

The R. & A. and USGA would like to record their appreciation of the valuable assistance which they have received from a number of golfing bodies throughout the world. The new Rules will become effective on 1st January 1988.

The combining of the Decisions Services of the R. & A. and USGA into a single volume has proved to be an outstanding success and has done much to establish uniformity of interpretation of the Rules worldwide.

We would like to take this opportunity to express our sincere thanks to our respective Committees and all those who have in so many ways helped us in our endeavours.

W. J. F. Bryce
Chairman
Rules of Golf Committee
Royal and Ancient Golf Club
of St. Andrews

C. Grant Spaeth
Chairman
Rules of Golf Committee
United States Golf Association

Contents

Changes

Principal Changes introduced in the 1988 Code

Rule 2.   Match Play
Expanded to state that a player may concede the next stroke, a hole or the match, and that a concession may not be declined or withdrawn.

Rule 3-3.   Stroke Play. Doubt as to Procedure
If a competitor fails to announce in advance his decision to invoke this Rule, the score with the original ball, rather than the higher score, will count.

Rule 4-4.   Maximum of Fourteen Clubs
Amended to state that a player may borrow a club from anyone on the course, but that the person from whom it was borrowed may not thereafter use the club.

Rule 5 and Appendix III
After 1st January 1990 it will no longer be permitted to use the small (1.620″) ball.

Rule 5-3.   Ball Unfit for Play
A stricter definition is adopted stating that a ball is unfit for play if it is visibly cut, cracked or out of shape, but a ball is not unfit for play solely because mud or other materials adhere to it, its surface is scratched or scraped or its paint is damaged or discoloured.

Rule 18.   Ball at Rest Moved
If a ball at rest moves after address (other than as a result of a stroke) the ball shall be replaced rather than played as it lies. This procedure is now consistent with that prescribed in other sub-sections of this Rule.

Rule 19-5.   Ball in Motion Deflected or Stopped by Another Ball
Clarifies that when two balls in motion collide, each player shall play his ball
as it lies.

**Rule 25-1b(ii) and 1c(ii).   Casual Water, Ground Under Repair and
Certain Damage to Course.   Relief.   In a Hazard**
Rule 26-1b.   Ball in Water Hazard
Rule 28c.   Ball Unplayable
Amended to state that the ball must be dropped keeping the point where
the ball lay (or where it last crossed the margin of the hazard, as the case
may be) between the spot on which the ball is dropped and the hole. It is no
longer permitted to stand on that line and drop a ball an arm's length to the
side.

The Rules of Golf

Section I   Etiquette

Courtesy on the Course

Safety

Prior to playing a stroke or making a practice swing, the player should
ensure that no one is standing close by or in a position to be hit by the club,
the ball or any stones, pebbles, twigs or the like which may be moved by the
stroke or swing.

Consideration for Other Players

The player who has the honour should be allowed to play before his
opponent or fellow-competitor tees his ball.

No one should move, talk or stand close to or directly behind the ball or
the hole when a player is addressing the ball or making a stroke.

In the interest of all, players should play without delay.

No player should play until the players in front are out of range.

Players searching for a ball should signal the players behind them to pass
as soon as it becomes apparent that the ball will not easily be found. They
should not search for five minutes before doing so. They should not
continue play until the players following them have passed and are out of
range.

When the play of a hole has been completed, players should immediately
leave the putting green.

Priority on the Course

In the absence of special rules, two-ball matches should have precedence
over and be entitled to pass any three- or four-ball match.

A single player has no standing and should give way to a match of any
kind.

Any match playing a whole round is entitled to pass a match playing a
shorter round.

If a match fails to keep its place on the course and loses more than one clear hole on the players in front, it should invite the match following to pass.

Care of the Course

Holes in Bunkers
Before leaving a bunker, a player should carefully fill up and smooth over all holes and footprints made by him.

Replace Divots; Repair Ball-Marks and Damage by Spikes
Through the green, a player should ensure that any turf cut or displaced by him is replaced at once and pressed down and that any damage to the putting green made by a ball is carefully repaired. Damage to the putting green caused by golf shoe spikes should be repaired *on completion of the hole*.

Damage to Greens – Flagsticks, Bags, etc.
Players should ensure that, when putting down bags or the flagstick, no damage is done to the putting green and that neither they nor their caddies damage the hole by standing close to it, in handling the flagstick or in removing the ball from the hole. The flagstick should be properly replaced in the hole before the players leave the putting green. Players should not damage the putting green by leaning on their putters, particularly when removing the ball from the hole.

Golf Carts
Local notices regulating the movement of golf carts should be strictly observed.

Damage Through Practice Swings
In taking practice swings, players should avoid causing damage to the course, particularly the tees, by removing divots.

Section II   Definitions

Addressing the Ball
A player has 'addressed the ball' when he has taken his stance and has also grounded his club, except that in a hazard a player has addressed the ball when he has taken his stance.
Advice
'Advice' is any counsel or suggestion which could influence a player in determining his play, the choice of a club or the method of making a stroke.

Information on the Rules or on matters of public information, such as the position of hazards or the flagstick on the putting green, is not advice.
Ball Deemed to Move   *see* 'Move or Moved'.
Ball Holed   *see* 'Holed'.
Ball Lost   *see* 'Lost Ball'.

Ball in Play
A ball is 'in play' as soon as the player has made a stroke on the <u>teeing ground</u>. It remains in play until holed out, except when it is <u>lost</u>, <u>out of bounds</u> or lifted, or another ball has been substituted under an applicable Rule, whether or not such Rule permits substitution; a ball so substituted becomes the ball in play.

Bunker
A 'bunker' is a <u>hazard</u> consisting of a prepared area of ground, often a hollow, from which turf or soil has been removed and replaced with sand or the like. Grass-covered ground bordering or within a bunker is not part of the bunker. The margin of a bunker extends vertically downwards, but not upwards.

Caddie
'A 'caddie' is one who carries or handles a player's clubs during play and otherwise assists him in accordance with the Rules.

When one caddie is employed by more than one player, he is always deemed to be the caddie of the player whose ball is involved, and <u>equipment</u> carried by him is deemed to be that player's equipment, except when the caddie acts upon specific directions of another player, in which case he is considered to be that other player's caddie.

Casual Water
'Casual water' is any temporary accumulation of water on the <u>course</u> which is visible before or after the player takes his <u>stance</u> and is not in a <u>water hazard</u>. Snow and ice are either casual water or loose impediments, at the option of the player, except that manufactured ice is an obstruction. Dew is not casual water.

Committee
The 'Committee' is the committee in charge of the competition or, if the matter does not arise in a competition, the committee in charge of the <u>course</u>.

Competitor
A 'competitor' is a player in a stroke competition. A 'fellow-competitor' is any person with whom the competitor plays. Neither is <u>partner</u> of the other.

In stroke play foursome and four-ball competitions, where the context so admits, the word 'competitor' or 'fellow-competitor' includes his partner.

Course
The 'course' is the whole area within which play is permitted (see Rule 33-2).

Equipment
'Equipment' is anything used, worn or carried by or for the player except any ball he has played at the hole being played and any small object, such as a coin or a tee, when used to mark the position of a ball or the extent of an area in which a ball is to be dropped. Equipment includes a golf cart, whether or not motorised. If such a cart is shared by more than one player, its status under the Rules is the same as that of a caddie employed by more than one player. See 'Caddie'.

Fellow-Competitor   *see* 'Competitor'.
Flagstick
The 'flagstick' is a movable straight indicator, with or without bunting or other material attached, centred in the hole to show its position. It shall be circular in cross-section.
Forecaddie
A 'forecaddie' is one who is employed by the Committee to indicate to players the position of balls during play. He is an <u>outside agency</u>.
Ground Under Repair
'Ground under repair' is any portion of the <u>course</u> so marked by order of the Committee or so declared by its authorised representative. It includes material piled for removal and a hole made by a greenkeeper, even if not so marked. Stakes and lines defining ground under repair are in such ground. The margin of ground under repair extends vertically downwards, but not upwards.

Note 1: Grass cuttings and other material left on the course which have been abandoned and are not intended to be removed are not ground under repair unless so marked.

Note 2: The Committee may make a Local Rule prohibiting play from ground under repair.
Hazards
A 'hazard' is any <u>bunker</u> or water <u>hazard</u>.
Hole
The 'hole' shall be 4¼ inches (108 mm) in diameter and at least 4 inches (100 mm) deep. If a lining is used, it shall be sunk at least 1 inch (25 mm) below the <u>putting green</u> surface unless the nature of the soil makes it impracticable to do so; its outer diameter shall not exceed 4¼ inches (108 mm).
Holed
A ball is 'holed' when it is at rest within the circumference of the hole and all of it is below the level of the lip of the hole.
Honour
The side entitled to play first from the <u>teeing ground</u> is said to have the 'honour'.
Lateral Water Hazard
A 'lateral water hazard' is a <u>water hazard</u> or that part of a water hazard so situated that it is not possible or is deemed by the Committee to be impracticable to drop a ball behind the water hazard in accordance with Rule 26-1b.

That part of a water hazard to be played as a lateral water hazard should be distinctively marked.

Note: Lateral water hazards should be defined by red stakes or lines.
Loose Impediments
'Loose impediments' are natural objects such as stones, leaves, twigs, branches and the like, dung, worms and insects and casts or heaps made by

them, provided they are not fixed or growing, are not solidly embedded and do not adhere to the ball.

Sand and loose soil are loose impediments on the <u>putting green</u>, but not elsewhere.

Snow and ice are either <u>casual water</u> or loose impediments, at the option of the player, except that manufactured ice is an <u>obstruction</u>.

Dew is not a loose impediment.

Lost Ball

A ball is 'lost' if:

a. It is not found or identified as his by the player within five minutes after the player's side or his or their caddies have begun to search for it; or

b. The player has put another ball into play under the Rules, even though he may not have searched for the original ball; or

c. The player has played any stroke with a <u>provisional ball</u> from the place where the original ball is likely to be or from a point nearer the hole than that place, whereupon the provisional ball becomes the <u>ball in play</u>.

Time spent in playing a <u>wrong ball</u> is not counted in the five-minute period allowed for search.

Marker

A 'marker' is one who is appointed by the Committee to record a <u>competitor's</u> score in stroke play. He may be a <u>fellow-competitor</u>. He is not a <u>referee</u>.

Matches *see* 'Sides and Matches'.

Move or Moved

A ball is deemed to have 'moved' if it leaves its position and comes to rest in any other place.

Observer

An 'observer' is one who is appointed by the Committee to assist a <u>referee</u> to decide questions of fact and to report to him any breach of a Rule. An observer should not attend the flagstick, stand at or mark the position of the hole, or lift the ball or mark its position.

Obstructions

An 'obstruction' is anything artificial, including the artificial surfaces and sides of roads and paths and manufactured ice, except:

a. Objects defining <u>out of bounds</u>, such as walls, fences, stakes and railings;

b. Any part of an immovable artificial object which is out of bounds; and

c. Any construction declared by the Committee to be an integral part of the course.

Out of Bounds

'Out of bounds' is ground on which play is prohibited.

When out of bounds is defined by reference to stakes or a fence or as being beyond stakes or a fence, the out of bounds line is determined by the nearest inside points of the stakes or fence posts at ground level excluding angled supports.

When out of bounds is defined by a line on the ground, the line itself is out of bounds.

The out of bounds line extends vertically upwards and downwards.

A ball is out of bounds when all of it lies out of bounds.

A player may stand out of bounds to play a ball lying within bounds.

Outside Agency

An 'outside agency' is any agency not part of the match or, in stroke play, not part of a competitor's side, and includes a referee, a marker, an observer or a forecaddie. Neither wind nor water is an outside agency.

Partner

A 'partner' is a player associated with another player on the same side.

In a threesome, foursome, best-ball or four-ball match, where the context so admits, the word 'player' includes his partner or partners.

Penalty Stroke

A 'penalty stroke' is one added to the score of a player or side under certain Rules. In a threesome or foursome, penalty strokes do not affect the order of play.

Provisional Ball

A 'provisional ball' is a ball played under Rule 27-2 for a ball which may be lost outside a water hazard or may be out of bounds.

Putting Green

The 'putting green' is all ground of the hole being played which is specially prepared for putting or otherwise defined as such by the Committee. A ball is on the putting green when any part of it touches the putting green.

Referee

A 'referee' is one who is appointed by the Committee to accompany players to decide questions of fact and apply the Rules of Golf. He shall act on any breach of a Rule which he observes or is reported to him.

A referee should not attend the flagstick, stand at or mark the position of the hole, or lift the ball or mark its position.

Rub of the Green

A 'rub of the green' occurs when a ball in motion is accidentally deflected or stopped by any outside agency (see Rule 19-1).

Rule

The term 'Rule' includes Local Rules made by the Committee under Rule 33-8a.

Sides and Matches

Side: A player, or two or more players who are partners.

Single: A match in which one plays against another.

Threesome: A match in which one plays against two, and each side plays one ball.

Foursome: A match in which two play against two, and each side plays one ball.

Three-ball: A match play competition in which three play against one another, each playing his own ball. Each player is playing two distinct matches.

Best-ball: A match in which one plays against the better ball of two or the best ball of three players.

Four-ball: A match in which two play their better ball against the better ball of two other players.

Stance

Taking the 'stance' consists in a player placing his feet in position for and preparatory to making a stroke.

Stipulated Round

The 'stipulated round' consists of playing the holes of the course in their correct sequence unless otherwise authorised by the Committee. The number of holes in a stipulated round is 18 unless a smaller number is authorised by the Committee. As to extension of stipulated round in match play, see Rule 2-3.

Stroke

A 'stroke' is the forward movement of the club made with the intention of fairly striking at and moving the ball, but if a player checks his downswing voluntarily before the clubhead reaches the ball he is deemed not to have made a stroke.

Teeing Ground

The 'teeing ground' is the starting place for the hole to be played. It is a rectangular area two club-lengths in depth, the front and the sides of which are defined by the outside limits of two tee-markers. A ball is outside the teeing ground when all of it lies outside the teeing ground.

Through the Green

'Through the green' is the whole area of the course except:

    a. The teeing ground and putting green of the hole being played; and

    b. All hazards on the course.

Water Hazard

A 'water hazard' is any sea, lake, pond, river, ditch, surface drainage ditch or other open water course (whether or not containing water) and anything of a similar nature.

All ground or water within the margin of a water hazard is part of the water hazard. The margin of a water hazard extends vertically upwards and downwards. Stakes and lines defining the margins of water hazards are in the hazards.

Note: Water hazards (other than lateral water hazards) should be defined by yellow stakes or lines.

Wrong Ball

A 'wrong ball' is any ball other than:

    a. The ball in play,

    b. A provisional ball or

    c. In stroke play, a second ball played under Rule 3-3 or Rule 20-7b.

Note: Ball in play includes a ball substituted for the ball in play when the player is proceeding under an applicable Rule which does not permit substitution.

Section III   The Rules of Play

THE GAME

Rule 1.   The Game

1-1.   General

The Game of Golf consists in playing a ball from the <u>teeing ground</u> into the hole by a <u>stroke</u> or successive strokes in accordance with the Rules.

1-2.   Exerting Influence on Ball

No player or caddie shall take any action to influence the position or the movement of a ball except in accordance with the Rules.

PENALTY FOR BREACH OF RULE 1-2:

Match play – Loss of hole; Stroke play – Two strokes.

Note: In the case of a serious breach of Rule 1-2, the Committee may impose a penalty of disqualification.

1-3   Agreement to Waive Rules

Players shall not agree to exclude the operation of any Rule or to waive any penalty incurred.

PENALTY FOR BREACH OF RULE 1-3:

Match play – Disqualification of both sides;

Stroke play – Disqualification of competitors concerned.

(Agreeing to play out of turn in stroke play – see Rule 10-2c.)

1-4.   Points Not Covered by Rules

If any point in dispute is not covered by the Rules, the decision shall be made in accordance with equity.

Rule 2.   Match Play

2-1.   Winner of Hole; Reckoning of Holes

In match play the game is played by holes.

Except as otherwise provided in the Rules, a hole is won by the side which holes its ball in the fewer strokes. In a handicap match the lower net score wins the hole.

The reckoning of holes is kept by the terms: so many 'holes up' or 'all square', and so many 'to play'.

A side is 'dormie' when it is as many holes up as there are holes remaining to be played.

2-2.   Halved Hole

A hole is halved if each side holes out in the same number of strokes.

When a player has holed out and his opponent has been left with a stroke for the half, if the player thereafter incurs a penalty, the hole is halved.

2-3. Winner of Match
A match (which consists of a stipulated round, unless otherwise decreed by the Committee) is won by the side which is leading by a number of holes greater than the number of holes remaining to be played.

The Committee may, for the purpose of settling a tie, extend the stipulated round to as many holes as are required for a match to be won.

2-4. Concession of Next Stroke, Hole or Match
When the opponent's ball is at rest or is deemed to be at rest under Rule 16-2, the player may concede the opponent to have holed out with his next stroke and the ball may be removed by either side with a club or otherwise.

A player may concede a hole or a match at any time prior to the conclusion of the hole or the match.

Concession of a stroke, hole or match may not be declined or withdrawn.

2-5. Claims
In match play, if a doubt or dispute arises between the players and no duly authorised representative of the Committee is available within a reasonable time, the players shall continue the match without delay. Any claim, if it is to be considered by the Committee, must be made before any player in the match plays from the next teeing ground or, in the case of the last hole of the match, before all players in the match leave the putting green.

No later claim shall be considered unless it is based on facts previously unknown to the player making the claim and the player making the claim had been given wrong information (Rules 6-2a and 9) by an opponent. In any case, no later claim shall be considered after the result of the match has been officially announced, unless the Committee is satisfied that the opponent knew he was giving wrong information.

2-6. General Penalty
The penalty for a breach of a Rule in match play is loss of hole except when otherwise provided.

Rule 3. Stroke Play

3-1. Winner
The competitor who plays the stipulated round or rounds in the fewest strokes is the winner.

3-2. Failure to Hole Out
If a competitor fails to hole out at any hole and does not correct his mistake before he plays a stroke from the next teeing ground or, in the case of the last hole of the round, before he leaves the putting green, *he shall be disqualified*.

3-3. Doubt as to Procedure
a. Procedure In stroke play only, when during play of a hole a competitor is doubtful of his rights or procedure, he may, without penalty, play a second ball. After the situation which caused the doubt has arisen, the

competitor should, before taking further action, announce to his marker or a fellow-competitor his decision to invoke this Rule and the ball with which he will score if the Rules permit.

The competitor shall report the facts to the <u>Committee</u> before returning his score card unless he scores the same with both balls; if he fails to do so, *he shall be disqualified.*

b. Determination of Score for Hole   If the Rules allow the procedure selected in advance by the competitor, the score with the ball selected shall be his score for the hole.

If the competitor fails to announce in advance his decision to invoke this Rule or his selection, the score with the original ball or, if the original ball is not one of the balls being played, the first ball into play shall count if the Rules allow the procedure adopted for such ball.

Note: A second ball played under Rule 3-3 is not a provisional ball under Rule 27-2.

3-4.   Refusal to Comply with a Rule
If a competitor refuses to comply with a Rule affecting the rights of another competitor, *he shall be disqualified.*

3-5.   General Penalty
The penalty for a breach of a Rule in stroke play is two strokes except when otherwise provided.

CLUBS AND THE BALL
The Royal and Ancient Golf Club of St. Andrews and the United States Golf Association reserve the right to change the Rules and make and change the interpretations relating to clubs, balls and other implements at any time.

Rule 4.   Clubs
If there may be any reasonable basis for doubt as to whether a club which is to be manufactured conforms with Rule 4 and Appendix II, the manufacturer should submit a sample to the Royal and Ancient Golf Club of St. Andrews for a ruling, such sample to become its property for reference purposes. If a manufacturer fails to do so, he assumes the risk of a ruling that the club does not conform with the Rules of Golf.

A player in doubt as to the conformity of a club should consult the Royal and Ancient Golf Club of St. Andrews.

4-1.   Form and Make of Clubs
A club is an implement designed to be used for striking the ball.

A putter is a club designed primarily for use on the putting green.

The player's clubs shall conform with the provisions of this Rule and with the specifications and interpretations set forth in Appendix II.

a. General   The club shall be composed of a shaft and a head. All parts of the club shall be fixed so that the club is one unit. The club shall not be designed to be adjustable except for weight. The club shall not be substantially different from the traditional and customary form and make.

b. Shaft The shaft shall be generally straight, with the same bending and twisting properties in any direction, and shall be attached to the clubhead at the heel either directly or through a single plain neck or socket. A putter shaft may be attached to any point in the head.

c. Grip The grip consists of that part of the shaft designed to be held by the player and any material added to it for the purpose of obtaining a firm hold. The grip shall be substantially straight and plain in form and shall not be moulded for any part of the hands.

d. Clubhead The distance from the heel to the toe of the clubhead shall be greater than the distance from the face to the back. The clubhead shall be generally plain in shape.

The clubhead shall have only one face designed for striking the ball, except that a putter may have two such faces if their characteristics are the same, they are opposite each other and the loft of each is the same and does not exceed ten degrees.

e. Club Face The face shall not have any degree of concavity and, in relation to the ball, shall be hard and rigid. It shall be generally smooth except for such markings as are permitted by Appendix II. If the basic structural material of the head and face of a club, other than a putter, is metal, no inset or attachment is permitted.

f. Wear A club which conforms to Rule 4-1 when new is deemed to conform after wear through normal use. Any part of a club which has been purposely altered is regarded as new and must conform, in the altered state, with the Rules.

g. Damage If a player's club ceases to conform with Rule 4-1 because of damage sustained in the normal course of play, the player may:

   (i)   use the club in its damaged state, but only for the remainder of the <u>stiplulated round</u> during which such damage was sustained;
       or

   (ii) without unduly delaying play, repair it.

A club which ceases to conform because of damage sustained other than in the normal course of play shall not subsequently be used during the round.

(Damage changing playing characteristics of club – see Rule 4-2.)

4-2. Playing Characteristics Changed

During a <u>stipulated round</u>, the playing characteristics of a club shall not be purposely changed.

If the playing characteristics of a player's club are changed during a round because of damage sustained in the normal course of play, the player may:

   (i)   use the club in its altered state; or

   (ii) without unduly delaying play, repair it.

If the playing characteristics of a player's club are changed because of damage sustained other than in the normal course of play, the club shall not subsequently be used during the round.

Damage to a club which occurred prior to a round may be repaired during the round, provided the playing characteristics are not changed and play is not unduly delayed.

4-3. Foreign Material
No foreign material shall be applied to the club face for the purpose of influencing the movement of the ball.

PENALTY FOR BREACH OF RULE 4-1, -2 or -3:
Disqualification.

4-4. Maximum of Fourteen Clubs
a. Selection and Replacement of Clubs   The player shall start a <u>stipulated round</u> with not more than fourteen clubs. He is limited to the clubs thus selected for that round except that, without unduly delaying play, he may:
  (i)   if he started with fewer than fourteen, add as many as will bring his total to that number; and
  (ii) replace, with any club, a club which becomes unfit for play in the normal course of play.

b. Borrowing or Sharing Clubs
The addition or replacement of a club or clubs may be made by borrowing from anyone; only the borrower may use such club or clubs for the remainder of the round.

The sharing of a club or clubs is prohibited except that partners may share clubs, provided that the total number of clubs carried by the partners so sharing does not exceed fourteen.

PENALTY FOR BREACH OF RULE 4-4a or b,
REGARDLESS OF NUMBER OF EXCESS CLUBS CARRIED:

Match play – At the conclusion of the hole at which the breach is discovered, the state of the match shall be adjusted by deducting one hole for each hole at which a breach occurred. Maximum deduction per round: two holes.

Stroke play – Two strokes for each hole at which any breach occurred; maximum penalty per round: four strokes.

Bogey and par competitions – Penalties as in match play.

Stableford competitions – see Note to Rule 32-1b.

c. Excess Club Declared Out of Play   Any club carried or used in breach of this Rule shall be declared out of play by the player immediately upon discovery that a breach has occurred and thereafter shall not be used by the player during the round.

PENALTY FOR BREACH OF RULE 4-4c:
Disqualification.

Rule 5.   The Ball

5-1.   General
The ball the player uses shall conform to specifications set forth in Appendix III on maximum weight, minimum size, spherical symmetry, initial velocity and overall distance when tested under specified conditions.

Note: In laying down the conditions under which a competition is to be played (Rule 33-1), the Committee may stipulate that the ball to be used shall be of certain specifications, provided these specifications are within the limits prescribed by Appendix III, and that it be of a size, brand and marking as detailed on the current List of Conforming Golf Balls issued by the Royal and Ancient Golf Club of St. Andrews.

5-2. Foreign Material

No foreign material shall be applied to a ball for the purpose of changing its playing characteristics.

PENALTY FOR BREACH OF RULE 5-1 or 5-2:
Disqualification.

5-3. Ball Unfit for Play

A ball is unfit for play if it is visibly cut, cracked or out of shape. A ball is not unfit for play solely because mud or other materials adhere to it, its surface is scratched or scraped or its paint is damaged or discoloured.

If a player has reason to believe his ball has become unfit for play during play of the hole being played, he may during the play of such hole lift his ball without penalty to determine whether it is unfit, provided he announces his intention in advance to his opponent in match play or his marker or a fellow-competitor in stroke-play and gives his opponent, marker or fellow-competitor an opportunity to examine the ball. If he lifts the ball without announcing his intention in advance or giving his opponent, marker or fellow-competitor an opportunity to examine the ball, *he shall incur a penalty of one stroke.*

If it is determined that the ball has become unfit for play during play of the hole being played, the player may substitute another ball, placing it on the spot where the original ball lay. Otherwise, the original ball shall be replaced.

If a ball breaks into pieces as a result of a stroke, the stroke shall be replayed without penalty (see Rule 20-5).

*PENALTY FOR BREACH OF RULE 5-3:
Match play – Loss of hole; Stroke play – Two strokes.

If a player incurs the general penalty for breach of Rule 5-3, no additional penalty under the Rule shall be applied.

Note 1: The ball may not be cleaned to determine whether it is unfit for play – see Rule 21.

Note 2: If the opponent, marker or fellow-competitor wishes to dispute a claim of unfitness, he must do so before the player plays another ball.

PLAYER'S RESPONSIBILITIES
Rule 6.   The Player

Definition

A 'marker' is one who is appointed by the Committee to record a competitor's score in stroke play. He may be a <u>fellow-competitor</u>. He is not a referee.

6-1.   Conditions of Competition
The player is responsible for knowing the conditions under which the competition is to be played (Rule 33-1).

6-2.   Handicap
a. Match Play   Before starting a match in a handicap competition, the players should determine from one another their respective handicaps. If a player begins the match having declared a higher handicap which would affect the number of strokes given or received, *he shall be disqualified*; otherwise, the player shall play off the declared handicap.
b. Stroke Play   In any round of a handicap competition, the competitor shall ensure that his handicap is recorded on his score card before it is returned to the Committee. If no handicap is recorded on his score card before it is recorded, or if the recorded handicap is higher than that to which he is entitled and this affects the number of strokes received, *he shall be disqualified* from that round of the handicap competition; otherwise, the score shall stand.
   Note: It is the player's responsibility to know the holes at which handicap strokes are to be given or received.

6-3.   Time of Starting and Groups
a. Time of Starting   The player shall start at the time laid down by the Committee.
b. Groups   In stroke play, the competitor shall remain throughout the round in the group arranged by the Committee unless the Committee authorises or ratifies a change.
   PENALTY FOR BREACH OF RULE 6-3: *Disqualification.*
   (Best-ball and four-ball play – see Rules 30-3a and 31-2.)
   Note: The Committee may provide in the conditions of a competition (Rule 33-1) that, if the player arrives at his starting point, ready to play, within five minutes after his starting time, in the absence of circumstances which warrant waiving the penalty of disqualification as provided in Rule 33-7, the penalty for failure to start on time is *loss of the first hole in match play or two strokes at the first hole in stroke play* instead of disqualification.

6-4.   Caddie
The player may have only one caddie at any one time, *under penalty of disqualification*.
   For any breach of a Rule by his caddie, the player incurs the relative penalty.

6-5.   Ball
The responsibility for playing the proper ball rests with the player. Each player should put an identification mark on his ball.

6-6.   Scoring in Stroke Play
a. Recording Scores   After each hole the marker should check the score with the competitor. On completion of the round the marker shall sign the

card and hand it to the competitor. If more than one marker records the scores, each shall sign for the part for which he is responsible.

b. Signing and Returning Card   After completion of the round, the competitor should check his score for each hole and settle any doubtful points with the Committee. He shall ensure that the marker has signed the card, countersign the card himself and return it to the Committee as soon as possible.

PENALTY FOR BREACH OF RULE 6-6b: *Disqualification.*

c. Alteration of Card   No alteration may be made on a card after the competitor has returned it to the Committee.

d. Wrong Score for Hole   The competitor is responsible for the correctness of the score recorded for each hole. If he returns a score for any hole lower than actually taken, *he shall be disqualified*. If he returns a score for any hole higher than actually taken, the score as returned shall stand.

Note 1: The Committee is responsible for the addition of scores and application of the handicap recorded on the card – see Rule 33-5.

Note 2: In four-ball stroke play, see also Rule 31-4 and -7a.

6-7.   Undue Delay
The player shall play without undue delay. Between completion of a hole and playing from the next teeing ground, the player shall not unduly delay play.

PENALTY FOR BREACH OF RULE 6-7:
Match play – Loss of hole; Stroke play – Two strokes.
For repeated offence – Disqualification.
If the player unduly delays play between holes, he is delaying the play of the next hole and the penalty applies to that hole.

6-8.   Discontinuance of Play
a. When Permitted   The player shall not discontinue play unless:
  (i)   the Committee has suspended play;
  (ii)   he believes there is danger from lightning;
  (iii) he is seeking a decision from the Committee on a doubtful or disputed point (see Rules 2-5 and 34-3); or
  (iv) there is some other good reason such as sudden illness.
  Bad weather is not of itself a good reason for discontinuing play.

If the player discontinues play without specific permission from the Committee, he shall report to the Committee as soon as practicable. If he does so and the Committee considers his reason satisfactory, the player incurs no penalty. Otherwise, *the player shall be disqualified*.

Exception in match play: Players discontinuing match play by agreement are not subject to disqualification unless by so doing the competition is delayed.

Note: Leaving the course does not of itself constitute discontinuance of play.

b. Procedure When Play Suspended by Committee   When play is suspended by the Committee, if the players in a match or group are between the play of two holes, they shall not resume play until the Committee has ordered a resumption of play. If they are in the process of playing a hole, they may continue provided they do so without delay. If they choose to continue, they shall discontinue either before or immediately after completing the hole, and shall not thereafter resume play until the Committee has ordered a resumption of play.

PENALTY FOR BREACH OF RULE 6-8b: Disqualification

c. Lifting Ball When Play Discontinued   When during the play of a hole a player discontinues play under Rule 6-8a, he may lift his ball. A ball may be cleaned when so lifted. If a ball has been so lifted, the player shall, when play is resumed, place a ball on the spot from which the original ball was lifted.

PENALTY FOR BREACH OF RULE 6-8c:
Match play – Loss of hole; Stroke play – Two strokes.

Rule 7.   Practice

7-1.   Before or Between Rounds

a. Match Play   On any day of a match play competition, a player may practise on the competition <u>course</u> before a round.

b. Stroke Play   On any day of a stroke competition or play-off, a competitor shall not practise on the competition <u>course</u> or test the surface of any putting green on the course before a round or play-off. When two or more rounds of a stroke competition are to be played over consecutive days, practice between those rounds on any competition course remaining to be played is prohibited.

Exception: Practice putting or chipping on or near the first <u>teeing ground</u> before starting a round or play-off is permitted.

PENALTY FOR BREACH OF RULE 7-1b: Disqualification.

Note: The Committee may in the conditions of a competition (Rule 33-1) prohibit practice on the competition course on any day of a match play competition or permit practice on the competition course or part of the course (Rule 33-2c) on any day of or between rounds of a stroke competition.

7-2.   During Round

A player shall not play a practice <u>stroke</u> either during the play of a hole or between the play of two holes except that, between the play of two holes, the player may practise putting or chipping on or near the <u>putting green</u> of the hole last played, any practice putting green or the <u>teeing ground</u> of the next hole to be played in the round, provided such practice stroke is not played from a hazard and does not unduly delay play (Rule 6-7).

Exception: When play has been suspended by the Committee, a player may, prior to resumption of play, practise (a) as provided in this Rule, (b) anywhere other than on the competition course and (c) as otherwise permitted by the Committee.

PENALTY FOR BREACH OF RULE 7-2:
Match play – Loss of hole; Stroke play – Two strokes.
In the event of a breach between the play of two holes, the penalty applies to the next hole.

Note 1: A practice swing is not a practice <u>stroke</u> and may be taken at any place, provided the player does not breach the Rules.

Note 2: The Committee may prohibit practice on or near the <u>putting green</u> of the hole last played.

Rule 8. Advice; Indicating Line of Play

Definition
'Advice' is any counsel or suggestion which could influence a player in determining his play, the choice of a club or the method of making a <u>stroke</u>.

Information on the Rules or on matters of public information, such as the position of hazards or the flagstick on the putting green, is not advice.

8-1. Advice
A player shall not give advice to anyone in the competition except his partner. A player may ask for advice from only his partner or either of their caddies.

8-2. Indicating Line of Play
a. Other Than on Putting Green Except on the <u>putting green</u>, a player may have the line of play indicated to him by anyone, but no one shall stand on or close to the line while the <u>stroke</u> is being played. Any mark placed during the play of a hole by the player or with his knowledge to indicate the line shall be removed before the stroke is played.

Exception: Flagstick attended or held up – see Rule 17-1.

b. On the Putting Green When the player's ball is on the <u>putting green</u>, the player, his partner or either of their caddies may, before but not during the <u>stroke</u>, point out a line for putting, but in so doing the putting green shall not be touched. No mark shall be placed anywhere to indicate a line for putting.

PENALTY FOR BREACH OF RULE:
Match play – Loss of hole; Stroke play – Two strokes.

Note: In a team competition without concurrent individual competition, the Committee may in the conditions of the competition (Rule 33-1) permit each team to appoint one person, e.g., team captain or coach, who may give <u>advice</u> (including pointing out a line for putting) to members of that team. Such person shall be identified to the Committee prior to the start of the competition.

Rule 9. Information as to Strokes Taken
9-1. General
The number of strokes a player has taken shall include any penalty strokes incurred.

9-2. Match Play

A player who has incurred a penalty shall inform his opponent as soon as practicable. If he fails to do so, he shall be deemed to have given wrong information, even if he was not aware that he had incurred a penalty.

An opponent is entitled to ascertain from the player, during the play of a hole, the number of strokes he has taken and, after play of a hole, the number of strokes taken on the hole just completed.

If during the play of a hole the player gives or is deemed to give wrong information as to the number of strokes taken, he shall incur no penalty if he corrects the mistake before his opponent has played his next stroke. If the player fails so to correct the wrong information, *he shall lose the hole*.

If after play of a hole the player gives or is deemed to give wrong information as to the number of strokes taken on the hole just completed and this affects the opponent's understanding of the result of the hole, he shall incur no penalty if he corrects his mistake before any player plays from the next <u>teeing ground</u> or, in the case of the last hole of the match, before all players leave the <u>putting green</u>. If the player fails so to correct the wrong information, *he shall lose the hole*.

9-3. Stroke Play

A competitor who has incurred a penalty should inform his marker as soon as practicable.

ORDER OF PLAY
Rule 10.   Order of Play

10-1.   Match Play

a. Teeing Ground   The side entitled to play first from the <u>teeing ground</u> is said to have the 'honour'.

The side which shall have the honour at the first teeing ground shall be determined by the order of the draw. In the absence of a draw, the honour should be decided by lot.

The side which wins a hole shall take the honour at the next teeing ground. If a hole has been halved, the side which had the honour at the previous teeing ground shall retain it.

b. Other Than on Teeing Ground   When the balls are in play, the ball farther from the hole shall be played first. If the balls are equidistant from the hole, the ball to be played first should be decided by lot.

Exception: Rule 30-3c (best-ball and four-ball match play).

c. Playing Out of Turn   If a player plays when his opponent should have played, the opponent may immediately require the player to cancel the stroke so played and play a ball in correct order, without penalty (see Rule 20-5).

10-2.   Stroke Play

a. Teeing Ground   The competitor entitled to play first from the <u>teeing ground</u> is said to have the 'honour'.

The competitor who shall have the honour at the first teeing ground shall be determined by the order of the draw. In the absence of a draw, the honour should be decided by lot.

The competitor with the lowest score at a hole shall take the honour at the next teeing ground. The competitor with the second lowest score shall play next and so on. If two or more competitors have the same score at a hole, they shall play from the next teeing ground in the same order as at the previous teeing ground.

b. Other Than on Teeing Ground When the balls are in play, the ball farthest from the hole shall be played first. If two or more balls are equidistant from the hole, the ball to be played first should be decided by lot.

Exceptions: Rules 22 (ball interfering with or assisting play) and 31-5 (four-ball stroke play).

c. Playing Out of Turn If a competitor plays out of turn, no penalty is incurred and the ball shall be played as it lies. If, however, the Committee determines that competitors have agreed to play in an order other than that set forth in Clauses 2a and 2b of this Rule to give one of them an advantage, *they shall be disqualified*.

(Incorrect order of play in threesomes and foursomes stroke play – see Rule 29-3.)

10-3. Provisional Ball or Second Ball from Teeing Ground

If a player plays a provisional ball or a second ball from a teeing ground, he should do so after his opponent or fellow-competitor has played his first stroke. If a player plays a provisional ball or a second ball out of turn, Clauses 1c and 2c of this Rule shall apply.

10-4. Ball Moved in Measuring

If a ball is moved in measuring to determine which ball is farther from the hole, no penalty is incurred and the ball shall be replaced.

TEEING GROUND
Rule 11. Teeing Ground

Definition

The 'teeing ground' is the starting place for the hole to be played. It is a rectangular area two club-lengths in depth, the front and the sides of which are defined by the outside limits of two tee-markers. A ball is outside the teeing ground when all of it lies outside the teeing ground.

11-1. Teeing

In teeing, the ball may be placed on the ground, on an irregularity of surface created by the player on the ground or on a tee, sand or other substance in order to raise it off the ground.

A player may stand outside the teeing ground to play a ball within it.

11-2 Tee-Markers

Before a player plays his first stroke with any ball from the teeing ground of the hole being played, the tee-markers are deemed to be fixed. In such circumstances, if the player moves or allows to be moved a tee-marker for the purpose of avoiding interference with his stance, the area of his intended swing or his line of play, *he shall incur the penalty for a breach of Rule 13-2.*

11-3 Ball Falling Off Tee
If a ball, when not in play, falls off a tee or is knocked off a tee by the player in addressing it, it may be re-teed without penalty, but if a stroke is made at the ball in these circumstances, whether the ball is moving or not, the stroke counts but no penalty is incurred.

11-4. Playing Outside Teeing Ground
a. Match Play If a player, when starting a hole, plays a ball from outside the teeing ground, the opponent may immediately require the player to cancel the stroke so played and play a ball from within the teeing ground, without penalty.

b. Stroke Play If a competitor, when starting a hole, plays a ball from outside the teeing ground, *he shall incur a penalty of two strokes* and shall then play a ball from within the teeing ground.

If the competitor plays a stroke from the next teeing ground without first correcting his mistake or, in the case of the last hole of the round, leaves the putting green without first declaring his intention to correct his mistake, *he shall be disqualified.*

Strokes played by a competitor from outside the teeing ground do not count in his score.

PLAYING THE BALL
Rule 12.   Searching for and Identifying Ball
Definitions
A 'hazard' is any bunker or water hazard.

A 'bunker' is a hazard consisting of a prepared area of ground, often a hollow, from which turf or soil has been removed and replaced with sand or the like. Grass-covered ground bordering or within a bunker is not part of the bunker. The margin of a bunker extends vertically downwards, but not upwards.

A 'water hazard' is any sea, lake, pond, river, ditch, surface drainage ditch or other open water course (whether or not containing water) and anything of a similar nature.

All ground or water within the margin of a water hazard is part of the water hazard. The margin of a water hazard extends vertically upwards and downwards. Stakes and lines defining the margins of water hazards are in the hazards.

12-1.   Searching for Ball; Seeing Ball
In searching for his ball anywhere on the course, the player may touch or bend long grass, rushes, bushes, whins, heather or the like, but only to the

extent necessary to find and identify it, provided that this does not improve the lie of the ball, the area of his intended swing or his line of play.

A player is not necessarily entitled to see his ball when playing a stroke.

In a <u>hazard</u>, if the ball is covered by <u>loose impediments</u> or sand, the player may remove by probing, raking or other means as much thereof as will enable him to see a part of the ball. If an excess is removed, no penalty is incurred and the ball shall be re-covered so that only a part of the ball is visible. If the ball is moved in such removal, no penalty is incurred; the ball shall be replaced and, if necessary, re-covered. As to removal of loose impediments outside a hazard, see Rule 23.

If a ball lying in <u>casual water</u>, <u>ground under repair</u> or a hole, cast or runway made by a burrowing animal, a reptile or a bird is accidentally moved during search, no penalty is incurred; the ball shall be replaced, unless the player elects to proceed under Rule 25-1b.

If a ball is believed to be lying in water in a <u>water hazard</u>, the player may probe for it with a club or otherwise. If the ball is moved in so doing, no penalty shall be incurred; the ball shall be replaced, unless the player elects to proceed under Rule 26-1.

PENALTY FOR BREACH OF RULE 12-1:
Match play – Loss of hole; Stroke play – Two strokes.

12-2. Identifying Ball

The responsibility for playing the proper ball rests with the player. Each player should put an identification mark on his ball.

Except in a <u>hazard</u>, the player may, without penalty, lift a ball he believes to be his own for the purpose of identification and clean it to the extent necessary for identification. If the ball is the player's ball, he shall replace it. Before the player lifts the ball, he shall announce his intention to his opponent in match play or his marker or a fellow-competitor in stroke play and give his opponent, marker or fellow-competitor an opportunity to observe the lifting and replacement. If he lifts his ball without announcing his intention in advance or giving his opponent, marker or fellow-competitor an opportunity to observe, or if he lifts his ball for identification in a hazard, *he shall incur a penalty of one stroke* and the ball shall be replaced.

If a player who is required to replace a ball fails to do so, *he shall incur the penalty* for a breach of Rule 20-3a, but no additional penalty under Rule 12-2 shall be applied.

Rule 13.   Ball Played As It Lies; Lie, Area of Intended Swing and Line of Play; Stance

Definitions

A 'hazard' is any <u>bunker</u> or <u>water hazard</u>.

A 'bunker' is a <u>hazard</u> consisting of a prepared area of ground, often a hollow, from which turf or soil has been removed and replaced with sand or the like. Grass-covered ground bordering or within a bunker is not part of the bunker. The margin of a bunker extends vertically downwards, but not upwards.

A 'water hazard' is any sea, lake, pond, river, ditch, surface drainage ditch or other open water course (whether or not containing water) and anything of a similar nature.

All ground or water within the margin of a water hazard is part of the water hazard. The margin of a water hazard extends vertically upwards and downwards. Stakes and lines defining the margins of water hazards are in the hazards.

13-1.   Ball Played As It Lies
The ball shall be played as it lies, except as otherwise provided in the Rules. (Ball at rest moved – Rule 18.)

13-2.   Improving Lie, Area of Intended Swing or Line of Play
Except as provided in the Rules, a player shall not improve or allow to be improved:

the position or lie of his ball,

the area of his intended swing,

his line of play or

the area in which he is to drop or place a ball

by any of the following actions:

moving, bending or breaking anything growing or fixed (including im-movable obstructions and objects defining out of bounds) or

removing or pressing down sand, loose soil, replaced divots, other cut turf placed in position or other irregularities of surface

except as follows:

as may occur in fairly taking his stance,

in making a stroke or the backward movement of his club for a stroke,

on the teeing ground in creating or eliminating irregularities of surface, or

on the putting green in removing sand and loose soil as provided in Rule 16-1a or in repairing damage as provided in Rule 16-1c.

The club may be grounded only lightly and shall not be pressed on the ground.

Exception: Ball lying in or touching hazard – see Rule 13-4.

13-3.   Building Stance
A player is entitled to place his feet firmly in taking his stance, but he shall not build a stance.

13-4.   Ball Lying in or Touching Hazard
Except as provided in the Rules, before making a stroke at a ball which lies in or touches a hazard (whether a bunker or a water hazard), the player shall not:

    a. Test the condition of the hazard or any similar hazard,

    b. Touch the ground in the hazard or water in the water hazard with a club or otherwise, or

c. Touch or move a <u>loose impediment</u> lying in or touching the hazard.
Exceptions:
1. At address or in the backward movement for the stroke, the club may touch any <u>obstruction</u> or any grass, bush, tree or other growing thing.
2. The player may place his clubs in a <u>hazard</u>, provided nothing is done which may constitute testing the soil or improving the lie of the ball.
3. The player after playing the stroke, or his <u>caddie</u> at any time without the authority of the player, may smooth sand or soil in the hazard, provided that, if the ball still lies in the hazard, nothing is done which improves the lie of the ball or assists the player in his subsequent play of the hole.

PENALTY FOR BREACH OF RULE:
Match play – Loss of hole; Stroke play – Two strokes.
(Searching for ball – see Rule 12-1.)

Rule 14.   Striking the Ball

Definition
A 'stroke' is the forward movement of the club made with the intention of fairly striking at and moving the ball, but if a player checks his downswing voluntarily before the clubhead reaches the ball he is deemed not to have made a stroke.

14-1.   Ball to be Fairly Struck At
The ball shall be fairly struck at with the head of the club and must not be pushed, scraped or spooned.

14-2.   Assistance
In making a stroke, a player shall not accept physical assistance or protection from the elements.

PENALTY FOR BREACH OF RULE 14-1 or -2:
Match play – Loss of hole; Stroke play – Two strokes.

14-3.   Artificial Devices and Unusual Equipment
Except as provided in the Rules, during a stipulated round the player shall not use any artificial device or unusual equipment:
a. For the purpose of gauging or measuring distance or conditions which might affect his play; or
b. Which might assist him in gripping the club, in making a stroke or in his play, except that plain gloves may be worn, resin, tape or gauze may be applied to the grip (provided such application does not render the grip non-conforming under Rule 4-1c) and a towel or handkerchief may be wrapped around the grip.

PENALTY FOR BREACH OF RULE 14-3: *Disqualification.*

14-4.   Striking the Ball More than Once
If a player's club strikes the ball more than once in the course of a <u>stroke</u>, the player shall count the stroke and *add a penalty stroke*, making two strokes in all.

14-5. Playing Moving Ball

A player shall not play while his ball is moving.

Exceptions:

Ball falling off tee – Rule 11-3.

Striking the ball more than once – Rule 14-4.

Ball moving in water – Rule 14-6.

When the ball begins to move only after the player has begun the stroke or the backward movement of his club for the stroke, he shall incur no penalty under this Rule for playing a moving ball, but he is not exempt from any penalty incurred under the following Rules:

Ball at rest moved by player – Rule 18-2a.

Ball at rest moving after address – Rule 18-2b.

Ball at rest moving after loose impediment touched – Rule 18-2c.

14-6. Ball Moving in Water

When a ball is moving in water in a <u>water hazard</u>, the player may, without penalty, make a <u>stroke</u>, but he must not delay making his stroke in order to allow the wind or current to improve the position of the ball. A ball moving in water in a water hazard may be lifted if the player elects to invoke Rule 26.

PENALTY FOR BREACH OF RULE 14-5 or -6:

Match play – Loss of hole; Stroke play – Two strokes.

Rule 15. Playing a Wrong Ball

Definition

A 'wrong ball' is any ball other than:

    a. The <u>ball in play</u>,

    b. A <u>provisional ball</u> or

    c. In stroke play, a second ball played under Rule 3-3 or Rule 20-7b.

Note: Ball in play includes a ball substituted for the ball in play when the player is proceeding under an applicable Rule which does not permit substitution.

15-1. General

A player must hole out with the ball played from the <u>teeing ground</u> unless a Rule permits him to substitute another ball. If a player substitutes another ball when proceeding under an applicable Rule which does not permit substitution, that ball is not a <u>wrong ball</u>; it becomes the <u>ball in play</u> and, if the error is not corrected as provided in Rule 20-6, *the player shall incur a penalty of loss of hole in match play or two strokes in stroke play*.

15-2. Match Play

If a player plays a stroke with a <u>wrong ball</u> except in a <u>hazard</u>, *he shall lose the hole*.

If a player plays any strokes in a hazard with a wrong ball, there is no penalty. Strokes played in a hazard with a wrong ball do not count in the player's score. If the wrong ball belongs to another player, its owner shall place a ball on the spot from which the wrong ball was first played.

If the player and opponent exchange balls during the play of a hole, the first to play the wrong ball other than from a hazard shall lose the hole; when this cannot be determined, the hole shall be played out with the balls exchanged.

15-3. Stroke Play

If a competitor plays a stroke or strokes with a <u>wrong ball</u>, *he shall incur a penalty of two strokes*, unless the only stroke or strokes played with such ball were played when it was lying in a hazard, in which case no penalty is incurred.

The competitor must correct his mistake by playing the correct ball. If he fails to correct his mistake before he plays a stroke from the next <u>teeing ground</u> or, in the case of the last hole of the round, fails to declare his intention to correct his mistake before leaving the <u>putting green</u>, *he shall be disqualified*.

Strokes played by a competitor with a wrong ball do not count in his score.

If the wrong ball belongs to another competitor, its owner shall place a ball on the spot from which the wrong ball was first played.

(Lie of ball to be placed or replaced altered – see Rule 20-3b.)

THE PUTTING GREEN
Rule 16. The Putting Green

Definitions

The 'putting green' is all ground of the hole being played which is specially prepared for putting or otherwise defined as such by the Committee. A ball is on the putting green when any part of it touches the putting green.

A ball is 'holed' when it is at rest within the circumference of the hole and all of it is below the level of the lip of the hole.

16-1. General

a. Touching Line of Putt The line of putt must not be touched except:
  (i) the player may move sand and loose soil on the putting green and other <u>loose impediments</u> by picking them up or by brushing them aside with his hand or a club without pressing anything down;
  (ii) in addressing the ball, the player may place the club in front of the ball without pressing anything down;
  (iii) in measuring – Rule 10-4;
  (iv) in lifting the ball – Rule 16-1b;
  (v) in pressing down a ball-marker;
  (vi) in repairing old hole plugs or ball marks on the putting green – Rule 16-1c; and
  (vii) in removing movable <u>obstructions</u> – Rule 24-1.
(Indicating line for putting on putting green – see Rule 8-2b.)

b. Lifting Ball   A ball on the <u>putting green</u> may be lifted and, if desired, cleaned. A ball so lifted shall be replaced on the spot from which it was lifted.

c. Repair of Hole Plugs and Ball Marks   The player may repair an old hole plug or damage to the <u>putting green</u> caused by the impact of a ball, whether or not the player's ball lies on the putting green. If the ball is moved in the process of such repair, it shall be replaced, without penalty.

d. Testing Surface   During the play of a hole, a player shall not test the surface of the <u>putting green</u> by rolling a ball or roughening or scraping the surface.

e. Standing Astride or on Line of Putt   The player shall not make a <u>stroke</u> on the <u>putting green</u> from a <u>stance</u> astride, or with either foot touching, the line of the putt or an extension of that line behind the ball. For the purpose of this Clause only, the line of putt does not extend beyond the hole.

f. Position of Caddie or Partner   While making the <u>stroke</u>, the player shall not allow his caddie, his partner or his partner's caddie to position himself on or close to an extension of the line of putt behind the ball.

g. Playing Stroke While Another Ball in Motion   A player shall not play a stroke while another ball is in motion after a stroke on the putting green.

(Lifting ball interfering with or assisting play while another ball in motion – see Rule 22.)

PENALTY FOR BREACH OF RULE 16-1:
Match play – Loss of hole; Stroke play – Two strokes.

16-2.   Ball Overhanging Hole   When any part of the ball overhangs the lip of the hole, the player is allowed enough time to reach the hole without unreasonable delay and an additional ten seconds to determine whether the ball is at rest. If by then the ball has not fallen into the hole, it is deemed to be at rest. If the ball subsequently falls into the hole, the player is deemed to have holed out with his last stroke, and *he shall add a penalty stroke to his score* for the hole; otherwise there is no penalty under this Rule.

(Undue delay – see Rule 6-7.)

Rule 17.   The Flagstick
17-1.   Flagstick Attended, Removed or Held Up

Before and during the <u>stroke</u>, the player may have the flagstick attended, removed or held up to indicate the position of the hole. This may be done only on the authority of the player before he plays his stroke.

If the flagstick is attended, removed or held up by an opponent, a fellow-competitor or the caddie of either with the player's knowledge and no objection is made, the player shall be deemed to have authorised it. If a player or a caddie attends, removes or holds up the flagstick or stands near the hole while a stroke is being played, he shall be deemed to be attending the flagstick until the ball comes to rest.

If the flagstick is not attended before the stroke is played, it shall not be attended or removed while the ball is in motion.

17-2. Unauthorised Attendance
a. Match Play In match play, an opponent or his caddie shall not attend, remove or hold up the flagstick without the player's knowledge or authority while the player is making a stroke or his ball is in motion.

b. Stroke Play In stroke play, if a fellow-competitor or his caddie attends, removes or holds up the flagstick without the competitor's knowledge or authority while the competitor is making a stroke or his ball is in motion, *the fellow-competitor shall incur the penalty* for breach of this Rule. In such circumstances, if the competitor's ball strikes the flagstick or the person attending it, the competitor incurs no penalty and the ball shall be played as it lies, except that, if the stroke was played from the putting green, the stroke shall be replayed.

PENALTY FOR BREACH OF RULE 17-1 or -2:
Match play – Loss of hole; Stroke play – Two strokes.

17-3. Ball Striking Flagstick or Attendant
The player's ball shall not strike:

a. The flagstick when attended, removed or held up by the player, his partner or either of their caddies, or by another person with the player's knowledge or authority; or

b. The player's caddie, his partner or his partner's caddie when attending the flagstick, or another person attending the flagstick with the player's knowledge or authority, or equipment carried by any such person; or

c. The flagstick in the hole, unattended, when the ball has been played from the putting green.

PENALTY FOR BREACH OF RULE 17-3:
Match play – Loss of hole; Stroke play – Two strokes,
and the ball shall be played as it lies.

17-4. Ball Resting Against Flagstick
If the ball rests against the flagstick when it is in the hole, the player or another person authorised by him may move or remove the flagstick and if the ball falls into the hole, the player shall be deemed to have holed out at his last stroke; otherwise the ball, if moved, shall be placed on the lip of the hole, without penalty.

BALL MOVED, DEFLECTED OR STOPPED
Rule 18. Ball at Rest Moved

Definitions
A ball is deemed to have 'moved' if it leaves its position and comes to rest in any other place.

An 'outside agency' is any agency not part of the match or, in stroke play, not part of a competitor's side, and includes a referee, a marker, an observer or a forecaddie. Neither wind nor water is an outside agency.

'Equipment' is anything used, worn or carried by or for the player except any ball he has played at the hole being played and any small object, such as a coin or a tee, when used to mark the position of a ball or the extent of an

132   *Golf*

area in which a ball is to be dropped. Equipment includes a golf cart, whether or not motorised. If such a cart is shared by more than one player, its status under the Rules is the same as that of a caddie employed by more than one player. See 'Caddie'.

A player has 'addressed the ball' when he has taken his <u>stance</u> and has also grounded his club, except that in a <u>hazard</u> a player has addressed the ball when he has taken his stance.

Taking the 'stance' consists in a player placing his feet in position for and preparatory to making a <u>stroke</u>.

18-1.   By Outside Agency
If a ball at rest is moved by an <u>outside agency</u>, the player shall incur no penalty and the ball shall be replaced before the player plays another <u>stroke</u>.

(Player's ball at rest moved by another ball – see Rule 18-5.)

18-2.   By Player, Partner, Caddie or Equipment
a.   General   When a player's ball is <u>in play</u>, if:
   (i)   the player, his partner or either of their caddies lifts or moves it, touches it purposely (except with a club in the act of addressing it) or causes it to move except as permitted by a Rule, or
   (ii)   equipment of the player or his partner causes the ball to move,
the player shall incur a penalty stroke. The ball shall be replaced unless the movement of the ball occurs after the player has begun his swing and he does not discontinue his swing.

Under the Rules no penalty is incurred if a player accidentally causes his ball to move in the following circumstances:

In measuring to determine which ball farther from hole – Rule 10-4
In searching for covered ball in <u>hazard</u> or for ball in <u>casual water</u>, <u>ground under repair</u>, etc. – Rule 12-1
In the process of repairing hole plug or ball mark – Rule 16-1c
In the process of removing <u>loose impediment</u> on <u>putting green</u> – Rule 18-2c
In the process of lifting ball under a Rule – Rule 20-1
In the process of placing or replacing ball under a Rule – Rule 20-3a
In complying with Rule 22 relating to lifting ball interfering with or assisting play
In removal of movable <u>obstruction</u> – Rule 24-1.

b.   Ball Moving After Address   If a player's <u>ball in play</u> <u>moves</u> after he has <u>addressed</u> it (other than as a result of a stroke), the player shall be deemed to have moved the ball and *shall incur a penalty stroke.* The player shall replace the ball unless the movement of the ball occurs after he has begun his swing and he does not discontinue his swing.

c.   Ball Moving After Loose Impediment Touched   <u>Through the green</u>, if the ball <u>moves</u> after any <u>loose impediment</u> lying within a club-length of it has been touched by the player, his partner or either of their caddies and before the player has <u>addressed</u> it, the player shall be deemed to have moved the ball and *shall incur a penalty stroke*. The player shall replace the ball unless the movement of the ball occurs after he has begun his swing and he does not discontinue his swing.

On the putting green, if the ball moves in the process of removing any loose impediment, it shall be replaced without penalty.

18-3. By Opponent, Caddie or Equipment in Match Play
a. During Search If, during search for a player's ball, it is moved by an opponent, his caddie or his equipment, no penalty is incurred and the player shall replace the ball.
b. Other Than During Search If, other than during search for a ball, the ball is touched or moved by an opponent, his caddie or his equipment, except as otherwise provided in the Rules, *the opponent shall incur a penalty stroke*. The player shall replace the ball.

(Ball moved in measuring to determine which ball farther from the hole – see Rule 10-4.)

(Playing a wrong ball – see Rule 15-2.)

(Ball moved in complying with Rule 22 relating to lifting ball interfering with or assisting play.)

18-4. By Fellow-Competitor, Caddie or Equipment in Stroke Play
If a competitor's ball is moved by a fellow-competitor, his caddie or his equipment, no penalty is incurred. The competitor shall replace his ball.

(Playing a wrong ball – see Rule 15-3.)

18-5. By Another Ball
If a ball in play and at rest is moved by another ball in motion after a stroke, the moved ball shall be replaced.

*PENALTY FOR BREACH OF RULE:

Match play – Loss of hole; Stroke play – Two strokes.

**If a player who is required to replace a ball fails to do so, he shall incur the general penalty for breach of Rule 18 but no additional penalty under Rule 18 shall be applied.*

Note 1: If a ball to be replaced under this Rule is not immediately recoverable, another ball may be substituted.

Note 2: If it is impossible to determine the spot on which a ball is to be placed, see Rule 20-3c.

Rule 19.   Ball in Motion Deflected or Stopped
Definitions
An 'outside agency' is any agency not part of the match or, in stroke play, not part of a competitor's side, and includes a referee, a marker, an observer or a forecaddie. Neither wind nor water is an outside agency.

'Equipment' is anything used, worn or carried by or for the player except any ball he has played at the hole being played and any small object, such as a coin or a tee, when used to mark the position of a ball or the extent of an area in which a ball is to be dropped. Equipment includes a golf cart, whether or not motorised. If such a cart is shared by more than one player, its status under the Rules is the same as that of a caddie employed by more than one player. See 'Caddie'.

19-1. By Outside Agency

If a ball in motion is accidentally deflected or stopped by any <u>outside agency</u>, it is a <u>rub of the green</u>, no penalty is incurred and the ball shall be played as it lies except:

    a. If a ball in motion after a <u>stroke</u> other than on the <u>putting green</u> comes to rest in or on any moving or animate outside agency, the player shall, <u>through the green</u> or in a <u>hazard</u>, drop the ball, or on the putting green place the ball, as near as possible to the spot where the outside agency was when the ball came to rest in or on it, and

    b. If a ball in motion after a stroke on the putting green is deflected or stopped by, or comes to rest in or on, any moving or animate outside agency except a worm or an insect, the stroke shall be cancelled and the ball shall be replaced.

    If the ball is not immediately recoverable, another ball may be substituted.

    (Player's ball deflected or stopped by another ball – see Rule 19-5.)

Note: If the referee or the Committee determines that a competitor's ball has been purposely deflected or stopped by an <u>outside agency</u>, Rule 1-4 applies to the competitor. If the outside agency is a fellow-competitor or his caddie, Rule 1-2 applies to the fellow-competitor.

19-2. By Player, Partner, Caddie or Equipment

a. Match Play   If a player's ball is deflected or stopped by himself, his partner or either of their caddies or <u>equipment</u>, *he shall lose the hole*.

b. Stroke Play   If a competitor's ball is deflected or stopped by himself, his partner or either of their caddies or <u>equipment</u>, *the competitor shall incur a penalty of two strokes*. The ball shall be played as it lies, except when it comes to rest in or on the competitor's, his partner's or either of their caddies' clothes or equipment, in which case the competitor shall <u>through the green</u> or in a <u>hazard</u> drop the ball, or on the <u>putting green</u> place the ball, as near as possible to where the article was when the ball came to rest in or on it.

    Exception: Dropped Ball – see Rule 20-2a.

    (Ball purposely deflected or stopped by player, partner or caddie – see Rule 1-2.)

19-3. By Opponent, Caddie or Equipment in Match Play

If a player's ball is accidentally deflected or stopped by an opponent, his caddie or his <u>equipment</u>, no penalty is incurred. The player may play the ball as it lies or, before another <u>stroke</u> is played by either side, cancel the stroke and replay it (see Rule 20-5). If the player elects to replay the stroke and the original ball is not immediately recoverable, another ball may be substituted.

If the ball has come to rest in or on the opponent's or his caddie's clothes or equipment, the player may <u>through the green</u> or in a <u>hazard</u> drop the ball, or on the putting green place the ball, as near as possible to where the article was when the ball came to rest in or on it.

Exception: Ball striking person attending flagstick – see Rule 17-3b.

(Ball purposely deflected or stopped by player, partner or caddie – see Rule 1-2).

19-4. By Fellow-Competitor, Caddie or Equipment in Stroke Play
See Rule 19-1 regarding ball deflected by outside agency.

19-5. By Another Ball
If a player's ball in motion after a stroke is deflected or stopped by a ball at rest, the player shall play his ball as it lies. In stroke play, if both balls lay on the <u>putting green</u> prior to the stroke, *the player incurs a penalty of two strokes*. Otherwise, no penalty is incurred.

If a player's ball in motion after a stroke is deflected or stopped by another ball in motion, the player shall play his ball as it lies. There is no penalty unless the player was in breach of Rule 16-1g, in which case *he shall incur the penalty for breach of that Rule*.

Exception: Ball in motion after a stroke on the putting green deflected or stopped by moving or animate outside agency – see Rule 19-1b.

PENALTY FOR BREACH OF RULE:
Match play – Loss of hole; Stroke play – Two strokes.

RELIEF SITUATIONS AND PROCEDURE
Rule 20. Lifting, Dropping and Placing;
Playing from Wrong Place

20-1. Lifting
A ball to be lifted under the Rules may be lifted by the player, his partner or another person authorised by the player. In any such case, the player shall be responsible for any breach of the Rules.

The position of the ball shall be marked before it is lifted under a Rule which requires it to be replaced. If it is not marked, *the player shall incur a penalty of one stroke* and the ball shall be replaced. If it is not replaced, *the player shall incur the general penalty* for breach of this Rule but no additional penalty under Rule 20-1 shall be applied.

If a ball or a ball-marker is accidentally moved in the process of lifting the ball under a Rule or marking its position, no penalty shall be incurred and the ball or ball marker shall be replaced.

Note: The position of a ball to be lifted should be marked by placing a ball-marker, a small coin or other similar object immediately behind the ball. If the ball-marker interferes with the play, <u>stance</u> or <u>stroke</u> of another player, it should be placed one or more clubhead-lengths to one side.

20-2. Dropping and Re-dropping
a. By Whom and How   A ball to be dropped under the Rules shall be

dropped by the player himself. He shall stand erect, hold the ball at shoulder height and arm's length and drop it. If a ball is dropped by any other person or in any other manner and the error is not corrected as provided in Rule 20-6, *the player shall incur a penalty stroke*.

If the ball touches the player, his partner, either of their caddies or their equipment before or after it strikes the ground, the ball shall be re-dropped, without penalty. There is no limit to the number of times a ball shall be re-dropped in such circumstances.

(Taking action to influence position or movement of ball – see Rule 1-2.)

b. Where to Drop   When a ball is to be dropped, it shall be dropped as near as possible to the spot where the ball lay, but not nearer the hole, except when a Rule permits or requires it to be dropped elsewhere. If a ball is to be dropped in a <u>hazard</u>, the ball shall be dropped in and come to rest in that hazard.

Note: A ball when dropped must first strike the ground where the applicable Rule requires it to be dropped. If it is not so dropped, Rules 20-6 and -7 apply.

c. When to Re-Drop   A dropped ball shall be re-dropped without penalty if it:

- (i)   rolls into a <u>hazard</u>;
- (ii)   rolls out of a hazard;
- (iii)   rolls onto a <u>putting green</u>;
- (iv)   rolls <u>out of bounds</u>;
- (v)   rolls back into the condition from which relief was taken under Rule 24-2 (immovable obstruction) or Rule 25 (abnormal ground conditions and wrong putting green);
- (vi)   rolls and comes to rest more than two club-lengths from where it first struck the ground; or
- (vii) rolls and comes to rest nearer the hole than its original position unless otherwise permitted by the Rules.

If the ball again rolls into such position, it shall be placed as near as possible to the spot where it first struck the ground when re-dropped.

If a ball to be re-dropped or placed under this Rule is not immediately recoverable, another ball may be substituted.

20-3.   Placing and Replacing

a. By Whom and Where   A ball to be placed under the Rules shall be placed by the player or his partner. A ball to be replaced shall be replaced by the player, his partner or the person who lifted or moved it. In any such case, the player shall be responsible for any breach of the Rules.

If a ball or a ball-marker is accidentally moved in the process of placing or replacing the ball, no penalty is incurred and the ball or the ball-marker shall be replaced.

b. Lie of Ball to Be Placed or Replaced Altered   If the original lie of a ball to be placed or replaced has been altered:

- (i)   except in a <u>hazard</u>, the ball shall be placed in the nearest lie most similar to the original lie which is not more than one club-length from the original lie, not nearer the hole and not in a hazard;

(ii) in a <u>water hazard</u>, the ball shall be placed in accordance with Clause (i) above, except that the ball must be placed in the water hazard;

(iii) In a <u>bunker</u>, the original lie shall be recreated as nearly as possible and the ball shall be placed in that lie.

c. Spot Not Determinable If it impossible to determine the spot where the ball is to be placed.

(i) <u>through the green</u>, the ball shall be dropped as near as possible to the place where it lay but not nearer the hole or in a <u>hazard</u>;

(ii) in a hazard, the ball shall be dropped in the hazard as near as possible to the place where it lay but not nearer the hole;

(iii) on the <u>putting green</u>, the ball shall be placed as near as possible to the place where it lay but not nearer the hole or in a hazard.

d. Ball Fails to Remain on Spot If a ball when placed fails to remain on the spot on which it was placed, it shall be replaced without penalty. If it still fails to remain on that spot.

(i) except in a <u>hazard</u>, it shall be placed at the nearest spot not nearer the hole or in a hazard where it can be placed at rest;

(ii) in a hazard, it shall be placed in the hazard at the nearest spot not nearer the hole where it can be placed at rest.

PENALTY FOR BREACH OF RULE 20-1, -2 or -3:
Match play – Loss of hole; Stroke play – Two strokes.

20-4. When Ball Dropped or Placed Is in Play

If the player's <u>ball in play</u> has been lifted, it is again in play when dropped or placed.

A substituted ball becomes the ball in play if it is dropped or placed under an applicable Rule, whether or not such Rule permits substitution. A ball substituted under an inapplicable Rule is a <u>wrong ball</u>.

20-5. Playing Next Stroke from Where Previous Stroke Played

When, under the Rules, a player elects or is required to play his next <u>stroke</u> from where a previous stroke was played, he shall proceed as follows: if the stroke is to be played from the <u>teeing ground</u>, the ball to be played shall be played from anywhere within the teeing ground and may be teed; if the stroke is to be played from <u>through the green</u> or a hazard, it shall be dropped; if the stroke is to be played on the <u>putting green</u>, it shall be placed.

PENALTY FOR BREACH OF RULE 20-5:
Match play – Loss of hole; Stroke play – Two strokes.

20-6. Lifting Ball Wrongly Dropped or Placed

A ball dropped or placed in a wrong place or otherwise not in accordance with the Rules but not played may be lifted, without penalty, and the player shall then proceed correctly.

20-7. Playing from Wrong Place
For a ball played outside teeing ground, see Rule 11-4.
a. Match Play If a player plays a stroke with a ball which has been dropped or placed in a wrong place, *he shall lose the hole*.
b. Stroke Play If a competitor plays a stroke with (i) his original ball which has been dropped or placed in a wrong place, (ii) a substituted ball which has been dropped or placed under an applicable Rule but in a wrong place or (iii) his ball in play when it has been moved and not replaced in a case where the Rules require replacement, *he shall*, provided a serious breach has not occurred, *incur the penalty prescribed by the applicable Rule* and play out the hole with the ball.

If, after playing from a wrong place, a competitor becomes aware of that fact and believes that a serious breach may be involved, he may, provided he has not played a stroke from the next teeing ground or, in the case of the last hole of the round, left the putting green, declare that he will play out the hole with a second ball dropped or placed in accordance with the Rules. The competitor shall report the facts to the Committee before returning his score card; if he fails to do so, *he shall be disqualified*. The Committee shall determine whether a serious breach of the Rule occurred. If so, the score with the second ball shall count and *the competitor shall add two penalty strokes to his score with that ball*.

If a serious breach has occurred and the competitor has failed to correct it as prescribed above, *he shall be disqualified*.

Note: If a competitor plays a second ball, penalty strokes incurred by playing the ball ruled not to count and strokes subsequently taken with that ball shall be disregarded.

Rule 21. Cleaning Ball
A ball on the putting green may be cleaned when lifted under Rule 16-1b. Elsewhere, a ball may be cleaned when lifted except when it has been lifted:
   a. To determine if it is unfit for play (Rule 5-3);
   b. For identification (Rule 12-2), in which case it may be cleaned only to the extent necessary for identification; or
   c. Because it is interfering with or assisting play (Rule 22).
If a player cleans his ball during play of a hole except as provided in this Rule, *he shall incur a penalty of one stroke* and the ball, if lifted, shall be replaced.

If a player who is required to replace a ball fails to do so, *he shall incur the penalty* for breach of Rule 20-3a, but no additional penalty under Rule 21 shall be applied.

Exception: If a player incurs a penalty for failing to act in accordance with Rule 5-3, 12-2 or 22, no additional penalty under Rule 21 shall be applied.

Rule 22. Ball Interfering with or Assisting Play
Any player may:
   a. Lift his ball if he considers that it might assist any other player or

b. Have any other ball lifted if he considers that it might interfere with his play or assist the play of any other player,

but this may not be done while another ball is in motion. In stroke play, a player required to lift his ball may play first rather than lift. A ball lifted under this Rule shall be replaced.

If a ball is accidentally moved in complying with this Rule, no penalty is incurred and the ball shall be replaced.

PENALTY FOR BREACH OF RULE:
Match play – Loss of hole; Stroke play – Two strokes.

Rule 23.   Loose Impediments

Definiton
'Loose impediments' are natural objects such as stones, leaves, twigs, branches and the like, dung, worms and insects and casts or heaps made by them, provided they are not fixed or growing, are not solidly embedded and do not adhere to the ball.

Sand and loose soil are loose impediments on the putting green but not elsewhere.

Snow and ice are either casual water or loose impediments, at the option of the player except that manufactured ice is an obstruction.

Dew is not a loose impediment.

23-1.   Relief
Except when both the loose impediment and the ball lie in or touch a hazard, any loose impediment may be removed without penalty. If the ball moves, see Rule 18-2c.

When a player's ball is in motion, a loose impediment on his line of play shall not be removed.

PENALTY FOR BREACH OF RULE:
Match play – Loss of hole; Stroke play – Two strokes.
(Searching for ball in hazard – see Rule 12-1.)
(Touching line of putt – see Rule 16-1a.)

Rule 24.   Obstructions

Definition
An 'obstruction' is anything artificial, including the artificial surfaces and sides of roads and paths and manufactured ice, except:

a. Objects defining out of bounds, such as walls, fences, stakes and railings;

b. Any part of an immovable artificial object which is out of bounds; and

c. Any construction declared by the Committee to be an integral part of the course.

24-1.   Movable Obstruction
A player may obtain relief from a movable obstruction as follows:

a. If the ball does not lie in or on the obstruction, the obstruction may be removed; if the ball moves, no penalty is incurred and the ball shall be replaced.

b. If the ball lies in or on the obstruction, the ball may be lifted, without penalty, and the obstruction removed. The ball shall <u>through the green</u> or in a <u>hazard</u> be dropped, or on the <u>putting green</u> be placed, as near as possible to the spot directly under the place where the ball lay in or on the obstruction, but not nearer the hole.

The ball may be cleaned when lifted for relief under Rule 24-1.

When a ball is in motion, an obstruction on the player's line of play other than an attended flagstick and equipment of the players shall not be removed.

24-2. Immovable Obstruction

a. Interference Interference by an immovable <u>obstruction</u> occurs when a ball lies in or on the obstruction, or so close to the obstruction that the obstruction interferes with the player's <u>stance</u> or the area of his intended swing. If the player's ball lies on the <u>putting green</u>, interference also occurs if an immovable obstruction on the putting green intervenes on his line of putt. Otherwise, intervention on the line of play is not, of itself, interference under this Rule.

b. Relief Except when the ball lies in or touches a <u>water hazard</u> or a <u>lateral water hazard</u>, a player may obtain relief from interference by an immovable <u>obstruction</u>, without penalty, as follows:

(i) **Through the Green:** If the ball lies <u>through the green</u>, the point on the course nearest to where the ball lies shall be determined (without crossing over, through or under the obstruction) which (a) is not nearer the hole, (b) avoids interference (as defined) and (c) is not in a <u>hazard</u> or on a <u>putting green</u>. The player shall lift the ball and drop it within one club-length of the point thus determined on ground which fulfils (a), (b) and (c) above.

Note: The prohibition against crossing over, through or under the <u>obstruction</u> does not apply to the artificial surfaces and sides of roads and paths or when the ball lies in or on the obstruction.

(ii) **In a Bunker:** If the ball lies in or touches a <u>bunker</u>, the player shall lift and drop the ball in accordance with Clause (i) above, except that the ball must be dropped in the bunker.

(iii) **On the Putting Green:** If the ball lies on the <u>putting green</u>, the player shall lift the ball and place it in the nearest position to where it lay which affords relief from interference, but not nearer the hole nor in a hazard.

The ball may be cleaned when lifted under Rule 24-2b.

(Ball rolling back into condition from which relief taken – see Rule 20-2c(v).)

Exception: A player may not obtain relief under Rule 24-2b if (a) it is clearly unreasonable for him to play a stroke because of interference by anything other than an immovable obstruction or (b) interference by an immovable obstruction would occur only through use of an unnecessarily abnormal stance, swing or direction of play.

Note: If a ball lies in or touches a <u>water hazard</u> (including a <u>lateral water hazard</u>), the player is not entitled to relief without penalty from interference by an immovable obstruction. The player shall play the ball as it lies or proceed under Rule 26-1.

PENALTY FOR BREACH OF RULE:
Match play – Loss of hole; Stroke play – Two strokes.

Rule 25.   Abnormal Ground Conditions
and Wrong Putting Green

Definitions

'Casual water' is any temporary accumulation of water on the <u>course</u> which is visible before or after the player takes his <u>stance</u> and is not in a <u>water hazard</u>. Snow and ice are either casual water or <u>loose impediments</u>, at the option of the player except that manufactured ice is an <u>obstruction</u>. Dew is not casual water.

'Ground under repair' is any portion of the <u>course</u> so marked by order of the Committee or so declared by its authorised representative. It includes material piled for removal and a hole made by a greenkeeper, even if not so marked. Stakes and lines defining ground under repair are in such ground. The margin of ground under repair extends vertically downwards, but not upwards.

Note 1: Grass cuttings and other material left on the course which have been abandoned and are not intended to be removed are not ground under repair unless so marked.

Note 2: The Committee may make a Local Rule prohibiting play from ground under repair.

25-1.   Casual Water, Ground Under Repair and Certain Damage to Course
a. Interference   Interference by <u>casual water</u>, <u>ground under repair</u> or a hole, cast or runway made by a burrowing animal, a reptile or a bird occurs when a ball lies in or touches any of these conditions or when the condition interferes with the player's <u>stance</u> or the area of his intended swing.

If the player's ball lies on the <u>putting green</u>, interference also occurs if such condition on the putting green intervenes on his line of putt.

If interference exists, the player may either play the ball as it lies (unless prohibited by Local Rule) or take relief as provided in Clause b.
b. Relief   If the player elects to take relief, he shall proceed as follows:
  (i)   **Through the Green:** If the ball lies <u>through the green</u>, the point on the <u>course</u> nearest to where the ball lies shall be determined which (a) is not nearer the hole, (b) avoids interference by the condition, and (c) is not in a <u>hazard</u> or on a <u>putting green</u>. The player shall lift the ball and drop it without penalty within one club-length of the point thus determined on ground which fulfils (a), (b) and (c) above.

(ii) **In a Hazard:** If the ball lies in or touches a <u>hazard</u>, the player shall lift and drop the ball either:

(a) Without penalty, in the hazard, as near as possible to the spot where the ball lay, but not nearer the hole, on ground which affords maximum available relief from the condition;

or

(b) *Under penalty of one stroke*, outside the hazard, keeping the point where the ball lay directly between the hole and the spot on which the ball is dropped.

Exception: If a ball lies in or touches a <u>water hazard</u> (including a <u>lateral water hazard</u>), the player is not entitled to relief without penalty from a hole, cast or runway made by a burrowing animal, a reptile or a bird. The player shall play the ball as it lies or proceed under Rule 26-1.

(iii) **On the Putting Green:** If the ball lies on the <u>putting green</u>, the player shall lift the ball and place it without penalty in the nearest position to where it lay which affords maximum available relief from the condition, but not nearer the hole nor in a <u>hazard</u>.

The ball may be cleaned when lifted under Rule 25-1b.

(Ball rolling back into condition from which relief taken – see Rule 20-2c(v).)

Exception: A player may not obtain relief under Rule 25-1b if (a) it is clearly unreasonable for him to play a stroke because of interference by anything other than a condition covered by Rule 25-1a or (b) interference by such a condition would occur only through use of an unnecessarily abnormal stance, swing or direction of play.

c. Ball Lost Under Condition Covered by Rule 25-1 It is a question of fact whether a ball lost after having been struck toward a condition covered by Rule 25-1 is lost under such condition. In order to treat the ball as lost under such condition, there must be reasonable evidence to that effect. In the absence of such evidence, the ball must be treated as a lost ball and Rule 27 applies.

(i) **Outside a Hazard** – If a ball is lost outside a <u>hazard</u> under a condition covered by Rule 25-1, the player may take relief as follows: the point on the <u>course</u> nearest to where the ball last crossed the margin of the area shall be determined which (a) is not nearer the hole than where the ball last crossed the margin, (b) avoids interference by the condition and (c) is not in a hazard or on a <u>putting green</u>. He shall drop a ball without penalty within one club-length of the point thus determined on ground which fulfils (a), (b) and (c) above.

(ii) **In a Hazard** – If a ball is lost in a <u>hazard</u> under a condition covered by Rule 25-1, the player may drop a ball either:

(a) Without penalty, in the hazard, as near as possible to the point at which the ball last crossed the margin of the area, but not nearer the hole, on ground which affords maximum available relief from the condition;

or
(b) *Under penalty of one stroke*, outside the hazard, keeping the
point at which the point at which the original ball last crossed the
margin of the hazard directly between the hole and the spot on
which the ball is dropped.

Exception: If a ball lies in a <u>water hazard</u> (including a <u>lateral water
hazard</u>), the player is not entitled to relief without penalty for a ball lost in a
hole, cast or runway made by a burrowing animal, a reptile or a bird. The
player shall proceed under Rule 26-1.

25-2. Embedded Ball
A ball embedded in its own pitch-mark in the ground in any closely mown
area <u>through the green</u> may be lifted, cleaned and dropped, without
penalty, as near as possible to the spot where it lay but not nearer the hole.
'Closely mown area' means any area of the <u>course</u>, including paths through
the rough, cut to fairway height or less.

25-3. Wrong Putting Green
If a ball lies on a <u>putting green</u> other than that of the hole being played, the
point on the <u>course</u> nearest to where the ball lies shall be determined which
(a) is not nearer the hole and (b) is not in a hazard or on a putting green. The
player shall lift the ball and drop it without penalty within one club-length
of the point thus determined on ground which fulfils (a) and (b) above. The
ball may be cleaned when so lifted.

Note: Unless otherwise prescribed by the Committee, the term 'a putting
green other than that of the hole being played' includes a practice putting
green or pitching green on the course.

PENALTY FOR BREACH OF RULE:
Match play – Loss of hole; Stroke play – Two strokes.

Rule 26.   Water Hazards
(Including Lateral Water Hazards)
Definitions
A 'water hazard' is any sea, lake, pond, river, ditch, surface drainage ditch
or other open water course (whether or not containing water) and anything
of a similar nature.

All ground or water within the margin of a water hazard is part of the
water hazard. The margin of a water hazard extends vertically upwards and
downwards. Stakes and lines defining the margins of water hazards are in
the hazards.

Note: Water hazards (other than <u>lateral water hazards</u>) should be defined
by yellow stakes or lines.

A 'lateral water hazard' is a <u>water hazard</u> or that part of a water hazard so
situated that it is not possible or is deemed by the Committee to be
impracticable to drop a ball behind the water hazard in accordance with
Rule 26-1b.

That part of a water hazard to be played as a lateral water hazard should be distinctively marked.

Note: Lateral water hazards should be defined by red stakes or lines.

26-1. Ball in Water Hazard
It a question of fact whether a ball lost after having been struck toward a <u>water hazard</u> is lost inside or outside the hazard. In order to treat the ball as lost in the hazard, there must be reasonable evidence that the ball lodged in it. In the absence of such evidence, the ball must be treated as a lost ball and Rule 27 applies.

If a ball lies in, touches or is lost in a water hazard (whether the ball lies in water or not), the player may *under penalty of one stroke*:

a. Play his next stroke as nearly as possible at the spot from which the original ball was last played (see Rule 20-5);
or

b. Drop a ball behind the water hazard, keeping the point at which the original ball last crossed the margin of the water hazard directly between the hole and the spot on which the ball is dropped, with no limit to how far behind the water hazard the ball may be dropped;
or

c. *As additional options available only if the ball lies in, touches or is lost in a lateral water hazard*, drop a ball outside the water hazard within two club-lengths of (i) the point where the original ball last crossed the margin of the water hazard or (ii) a point on the opposite margin of the water hazard equidistant from the hole. The ball must be dropped and come to rest not nearer the hole than the point where the original ball last crossed the margin of the water hazard.

The ball may be cleaned when lifted under this Rule.

(Ball moving in water in a water hazard – see Rule 14-6.)

26-2. Ball Played Within Water Hazard
a. Ball Comes to Rest in Hazard If a ball played from within a water hazard comes to rest in the hazard after the stroke, the player may:
  (i) proceed under Rule 26-1; or
  (ii) *under penalty of one stroke*, play his next stroke as nearly as possible at the spot from which the last stroke from outside the hazard was played (see Rule 20-5).

b. Ball Lost or Unplayable Outside Hazard or Out of Bounds If a ball played from within a water hazard is lost or declared unplayable outside the hazard or is out of bounds, the player, after taking *a penalty of one stroke* under Rule 27-1 or 28a, may:
  (i) play a ball as nearly as possible at the spot in the hazard from which the original ball was last played (see Rule 20-5); or
  (ii) *under an additional penalty of one stroke* Rule 26-1b or, if applicable, Rule 26-1c, using as the reference point the point where the original ball last crossed the margin of the hazard before it came to rest in the hazard; or

(iii) *under an additional penalty of one stroke*, play his next stroke as nearly as possible at the spot from which the last stroke from outside the hazard was played (see Rule 20-5).

Note: If a ball played from within a water hazard is declared unplayable outside the hazard, nothing in Rule 26-2b precludes the player from proceeding under Rule 28b or c.

PENALTY FOR BREACH OF RULE:
Match play – Loss of hole; Stroke play – Two strokes.

Rule 27.   Ball Lost or Out of Bounds; Provisional Ball

If the original ball is lost under a condition covered by Rule 25-1 (casual water, ground under repair and certain damage to the course), the player may proceed under that Rule. If the original ball is lost in a water hazard, the player shall proceed under Rule 26.

Such Rules may not be used unless there is reasonable evidence that the ball is lost under a condition covered by Rule 25-1 or in a water hazard.

Definitions

A ball is 'lost' if:

a. It is not found or identified as his by the player within five minutes after the player's side or his or their caddies have begun to search for it; or

b. The player has put another ball into play under the Rules, even though he may not have searched for the original ball; or

c. The player has played any stroke with a provisional ball from the place where the original ball is likely to be or from a point nearer the hole than that place, whereupon the provisional ball becomes the ball in play.

Time spent in playing a wrong ball is not counted in the five-minute period allowed for search.

'Out of bounds' is ground on which play is prohibited.

When out of bounds is defined by reference to stakes or a fence, or as being beyond stakes or a fence, the out of bounds line is determined by the nearest inside points of the stakes or fence posts at ground level excluding angled supports.

When out of bounds is defined by a line on the ground, the line itself is out of bounds.

The out of bounds line extends vertically upwards and downwards.

A ball is out of bounds when all of it lies out of bounds.

A player may stand out of bounds to play a ball lying within bounds.

A 'provisional ball' is a ball played under Rule 27-2 for a ball which may be lost outside a water hazard or may be out of bounds.

27-1.   Ball Lost or Out of Bounds

If a ball is lost outside a water hazard or is out of bounds, the player shall play a ball, *under penalty of one stroke*, as nearly as possible at the spot from which the original ball was last played or moved by him (see Rule 20-5).

PENALTY FOR BREACH OF RULE 27-1:
Match play – Loss of hole; Stroke play – Two strokes.

27-2. Provisional Ball

a. Procedure If a ball may be <u>lost</u> outside a <u>water hazard</u> or may be <u>out of bounds</u>, to save time the player may play another ball provisionally as nearly as possible at the spot from which the original ball was played (see Rule 20-5). The player shall inform his opponent in match play or his marker or a fellow competitor in stroke play that he intends to play a <u>provisional ball</u>, and he shall play it before he or his partner goes forward to search for the original ball. If he fails to do so and plays another ball, such ball is not a provisional ball and becomes the <u>ball in play</u> *under penalty of stroke and distance* (Rule 27-1); the original ball is deemed to be lost.

b. When Provisional Ball Becomes Ball in Play The player may play a provisional ball until he reaches the place where the original ball is likely to be. If he plays a stroke with the provisional ball from the place where the original ball is likely to be or from a point nearer the hole than that place, the original ball is deemed to be <u>lost</u> and the provisional ball becomes the ball in play under *penalty of stroke and distance* (Rule 27-1).

If the original ball is lost outside a water hazard or is out of bounds, the provisional ball becomes the ball in play, *under penalty of stroke and distance* (Rule 27-1).

c. When Provisional Ball to Be Abandoned If the original ball is neither lost outside a water hazard nor out of bounds, the player shall abandon the provisional ball and continue play with the original ball. If he fails to do so, any further strokes played with the provisional ball shall constitute playing a <u>wrong ball</u> and the provisions of Rule 15 shall apply.

Note: If the original ball lies in a water hazard, the player shall play the ball as it lies or proceed under Rule 26. If it is lost in a water hazard or unplayable, the player shall proceed under Rule 26 or 28, whichever is applicable.

Rule 28. Ball Unplayable

The player may declare his ball unplayable at any place on the course except when the ball lies in or touches a <u>water hazard</u>. The player is the sole judge as to whether his ball is unplayable.

If the player deems his ball to be unplayable, he shall, *under penalty of one stroke*:

a. Play his next stroke as nearly as possible at the spot from which the original ball was last played (see Rule 20-5);

or

b. Drop a ball within two club-lengths of the spot where the ball lay, but not nearer the hole;

or

c. Drop a ball behind the point where the ball lay, keeping that point directly between the hole and the spot on which the ball is dropped, with no limit to how far behind that point the ball may be dropped.

If the unplayable ball lies in a <u>bunker</u> and the player elects to proceed under Clause b or c, a ball must be dropped in the bunker.

The ball may be cleaned when lifted under this Rule.
PENALTY FOR BREACH OF RULE:
Match play – Loss of hole; Stroke play – Two strokes.

OTHER FORMS OF PLAY
Rule 29.   Threesomes and Foursomes
Definitions

Threesome: A match in which one plays against two, and each side plays one ball.

Foursome: A match in which two play against two, and each side plays one ball.

29-1.   General
In a threesome or a foursome, during any <u>stipulated round</u> the partners shall play alternately from the teeing grounds and alternately during the play of each hole. <u>Penalty strokes</u> do not affect the order of play.

29-2.   Match Play
If a player plays when his partner should have played, *his side shall lose the hole.*

29-3.   Stroke Play
If the partners play a stroke or strokes in incorrect order, such stroke or strokes shall be cancelled and *the side shall incur a penalty of two strokes.* The side shall correct the error by playing a ball in correct order at the spot from which it first played in incorrect order (see Rule 20-5). If the side plays a stroke from the next <u>teeing ground</u> without first correcting the error or, in the case of the last hole of the round, leaves the <u>putting green</u> without declaring its intention to correct the error, *the side shall be disqualified.*

Rule 30.   Three-Ball, Best-Ball and Four-Ball Match Play
Definitions

Three-Ball: A match play competition in which three play against one another, each playing his own ball. Each player is playing two distinct matches.

Best-Ball: A match in which one plays against the better ball of two or the best ball of three players.

Four-Ball: A match in which two play their better ball against the better ball of two other players.

30-1.   Rules of Golf Apply
The Rules of Golf, so far as they are not at variance with the following special Rules, shall apply to three-ball, best-ball and four-ball matches.

30-2.   Three-Ball Match Play
a. Ball at Rest Moved by an Opponent   Except as otherwise provided in

the Rules, if the player's ball is touched or moved by an opponent, his caddie or equipment other than during search, Rule 18-3b applies. *That opponent shall incur a penalty stroke in his match with the player*, but not in his match with the other opponent.

b. Ball Deflected or Stopped by an Opponent Accidentally If a player's ball is accidentally deflected or stopped by an opponent, his caddie or equipment, no penalty shall be incurred. In his match with that opponent the player may play the ball as it lies or, before another stroke is played by either side, he may cancel the stroke and replay it (see Rule 20-5). In his match with the other opponent, the ball shall be played as it lies.

Exception: Ball striking person attending flagstick – see Rule 17-3b.

(Ball purposely deflected or stopped by opponent – see Rule 1-2.)

30-3.   Best-Ball and Four-Ball Match Play

a. Representation of Side A side may be represented by one partner for all or any part of a match; all partners need not be present. An absent partner may join a match between holes, but not during play of a hole.

b. Maximum of Fourteen Clubs *The side shall be penalised* for a breach of Rule 4-4 by any partner.

c. Order of Play Balls belonging to the same side may be played in the order the side considers best.

d. Wrong Ball If a player plays a stroke with a wrong ball except in a hazard, *he shall be disqualified for that hole*, but his partner incurs no penalty even if the wrong ball belongs to him. The owner of the ball shall replace it on the spot from which it was played, without penalty. If the ball is not immediately recoverable, another ball may be substituted.

e. Disqualification of Side
  (i) *A side shall be disqualified* for a breach of any of the following by any partner:

Rule 1-3 –	Agreement to Waive Rules.
Rule 4-1, -2 or -3 –	Clubs.
Rule 5-1, -2 –	The Ball.
Rule 6-2a –	Handicap (playing off higher handicap).
Rule 6-4 –	Caddie.
Rule 6-7 –	Undue Delay (repeated offence).
Rule 14-3 –	Artificial Devices and Unusual Equipment.

  (ii) *A side shall be disqualified* for a breach of any of the following by all partners:

Rule 6-3 –	Time of Starting and Groups.
Rule 6-8 –	Discontinuance of Play.

f. Effect of Other Penalties If a player's breach of a Rule assists his partner's play or adversely affects an opponent's play, *the partner incurs the applicable penalty in addition to any penalty incurred by the player*.

In all other cases where a player incurs a penalty for breach of a Rule, the penalty shall not apply to his partner. Where the penalty is stated to be loss of hole, the effect shall be to disqualify the player for that hole.

g. Another Form of Match Played Concurrently In a best-ball or four-ball match when another form of match is played concurrently, the above special Rules shall apply.

Rule 31.   Four-Ball Stroke Play

In four-ball stroke play two competitors play as partners, each playing his own ball. The lower score of the partners is the score for the hole. If one partner fails to complete the play of a hole, there is no penalty.

31-1.   Rules of Golf Apply

The Rules of Golf, so far as they are not at variance with the following special Rules, shall apply to four-ball stroke play.

31-2.   Representation of Side

A side may be represented by either partner for all or any part of a stipulated round; both partners need not be present. An absent competitor may join his partner between holes, but not during play of a hole.

31-3.   Maximum of Fourteen Clubs

The side shall be penalised for a breach of Rule 4-4 by either partner.

31-4.   Scoring

The marker is required to record for each hole only the gross score of whichever partner's score is to count. The gross scores to count must be individually identifiable; otherwise *the side shall be disqualified.* Only one of the partners need be responsible for complying with Rule 6-6b.

   (Wrong score – see Rule 31-7a.)

31-5.   Order of Play

Balls belonging to the same side may be played in the order the side considers best.

31-6.   Wrong Ball

If a competitor plays a stroke with a wrong ball except in a hazard, *he shall add two penalty strokes to his score for the hole* and shall then play the correct ball. His partner incurs no penalty even if the wrong ball belongs to him.

   The owner of the ball shall replace it on the spot from which it was played, without penalty. If the ball is not immediately recoverable, another ball may be substituted.

31-7.   Disqualification Penalties

a. Breach by One Partner *A side shall be disqualified from the competition* for a breach of any of the following by either partner:

Rule 1-3 –	Agreement to Waive Rules.
Rule 3-4 –	Refusal to Comply with Rule.
Rule 4-1, -2 or -3 –	Clubs.
Rule 5-1 or -2 –	The Ball.
Rule 6-2b –	Handicap (playing off higher handicap; failure to record handicap).

Rule 6-4 –	Caddie.
Rule 6-6b –	Signing and Returning Card.
Rule 6-6c –	Wrong Score for Hole, i.e. when the recorded lower score of the partners is lower than actually taken. If the recorded lower score of the partners is higher than actually taken, it must stand as returned.
Rule 6-7 –	Undue Delay (repeated offence).
Rule 7-1 –	Practice Before or Between Rounds.
Rule 14-3 –	Artificial Devices and Unusual Equipment.
Rule 31-4 –	Gross Scores to count Not Individually Identifiable.

b. Breach by Both Partners *A side shall be disqualified:*

(i) for a breach by both partners of Rule 6-3 (Time of Starting and Groups) or Rule 6-8 (Discontinuance of Play), or

(ii) if, at the same hole, each partner is in breach of a Rule the penalty for which is disqualification from the competition or for a hole.

c. For the Hole Only   In all other cases where a breach of a Rule would entail disqualification, *the competitor shall be disqualified only for the hole at which the breach occurred*.

31-8.   Effect of Other Penalties

If a competitor's breach of a Rule assists his partner's play, *the partner incurs the applicable penalty in addition to any penalty incurred by the competitor*.

In all other cases where a competitor incurs a penalty for breach of a Rule, the penalty shall not apply to his partner.

Rule 32.   Bogey, Par and Stableford Competitions

32-1.   Conditions

Bogey, par and Stableford competitions are forms of stroke competition in which play is against a fixed score at each hole. The Rules for stroke play, so far as they are not at variance with the following special Rules, apply.

a. Bogey and Par Competitions   The reckoning for bogey and par competitions is made as in match play. Any hole for which a competitor makes no return shall be regarded as a loss. The winner is the competitor who is most successful in the aggregate of holes.

The marker is responsible for marking only the gross number of strokes for each hole where the competitor makes a net score equal to or less than the fixed score.

Note: Maximum of 14 Clubs – Penalties as in match play – see Rule 4-4.

b. Stableford Competitions   The reckoning in Stableford competitions is made by points awarded in relation to a fixed score at each hole as follows:

Hole Played in	Points
More than one over fixed score or no score returned	0
One over fixed score	1
Fixed score	2
One under fixed score	3

Two under fixed score 4
Three under fixed score 5

The winner is the competitor who scores the highest number of points.

The marker shall be responsible for marking only the gross number of strokes at each hole where the competitor's net score earns one or more points.

Note: Maximum of 14 Clubs (Rule 4-4) – Penalties applied as follows: From total points scored for the round, deduction of two points for each hole at which any breach occurred; maximum deduction per round: four points.

32-2. Disqualification Penalties

a. From the Competition *A competitor shall be disqualified* from the competition for a breach of any of the following:

Rule 1-3 –	Agreement to Waive Rules.
Rule 3-4 –	Refusal to Comply with Rule.
Rule 4-1, -2 or -3 –	Clubs.
Rule 5-1 or -2 –	The Ball.
Rule 6-2b –	Handicap (playing off higher handicap; failure to record handicap).
Rule 6-3 –	Time of Starting and Groups.
Rule 6-4 –	Caddie.
Rule 6-6b –	Signing and Returning Card.
Rule 6-6d –	Wrong Score for Hole, except that no penalty shall be incurred when a breach of this Rule does not affect the result of the hole.
Rule 6-7 –	Undue Delay (repeated offence).
Rule 6-8 –	Discontinuance of Play.
Rule 7-1 –	Practice Before or Between Rounds.
Rule 14-3 –	Artificial Devices and Unusual Equipment.

b. For a Hole In all other cases where a breach of a Rule would entail disqualification, *the competitor shall be disqualified only for the hole at which the breach occurred.*

ADMINISTRATION
Rule 33.   The Committee
33-1. Conditions; Waiving Rule

The Committee shall lay down the conditions under which a competition is to be played.

The Committee has no power to waive a Rule of Golf.

Certain special rules governing stroke play are so substantially different from those governing match play that combining the two forms of play is not practicable and is not permitted. The results of matches played and the scores returned in these circumstances shall not be accepted.

In stroke play the Committee may limit a referee's duties.

33-2.   The Course

a. Defining Bounds and Margins   The Committee shall define accurately:
  (i)   the course and out of bounds,
  (ii)   the margins of water hazards and lateral water hazards,
  (iii) ground under repair, and
  (iv)   obstructions and integral parts of the course.

b. New Holes   New holes should be made on the day on which a stroke competition begins and at such other times as the Committee considers necessary, provided all competitors in a single round play with each hole cut in the same position.

Exception: When it is impossible for a damaged hole to be repaired so that it conforms with the Definition, the Committee may make a new hole in a nearby similar position.

c. Practice Ground   Where there is no practice ground available outside the area of a competition course, the Committee should lay down the area on which players may practise on any day of a competition, if it is practicable to do so. On any day of a stroke competition, the Committee should not normally permit practice on or to a putting green or from a hazard of the competition course.

d. Course Unplayable   If the Committee or its authorised representative considers that for any reason the course is not in a playable condition or that there are circumstances which render the proper playing of the game impossible, it may, in match play or stroke play, order a temporary suspension of play or, in stroke play, declare play null and void and cancel all scores for the round in question. When play has been temporarily suspended, it shall be resumed from where it was discontinued, even though resumption occurs on a subsequent day. When a round is cancelled, all penalties incurred in that round are cancelled.

(Procedure in discontinuing play – see Rule 6-8.)

33-3.   Times of Starting and Groups

The Committee shall lay down the times of starting and, in stroke play, arrange the groups in which competitors shall play.

When a match play competition is played over an extended period, the Committee shall lay down the limit of time within which each round shall be completed. When players are allowed to arrange the date of their match within these limits, the Committee should announce that the match must be played at a stated time on the last day of the period unless the players agree to a prior date.

33-4.   Handicap Stroke Table

The Committee shall publish a table indicating the order of holes at which handicap strokes are to be given or received.

33-5.   Score Card

In stroke play, the Committee shall issue for each competitor a score card containing the date and the competitor's name or, in foursome or four-ball stroke play, the competitors' names.

In stroke play, the Committee is responsible for the addition of scores and application of the handicap recorded on the card.

In four-ball stroke play, the Committee is responsible for recording the better-ball score for each hole and in the process applying the handicaps recorded on the card, and adding the better-ball scores.

33-6. Decision of Ties

The Committee shall announce the manner, day and time for the decision of a halved match or of a tie, whether played on level terms or under handicap.

A halved match shall not be decided by stroke play. A tie in stroke play shall not be decided by a match.

33-7. Disqualification Penalty; Committee Discretion

A penalty of disqualification may in exceptional individual cases be waived, modified or imposed if the Committee considers such action warranted.

33-8. Local Rules

a. Policy The Committee may make and publish Local Rules for abnormal conditions if they are consistent with the policy of the Governing Authority for the country concerned as set forth in Appendix I to these Rules.

b. Waiving Penalty A penalty imposed by a Rule of Golf shall not be waived by a Local Rule.

Rule 34. Disputes and Decisions

34-1. Claims and Penalties

a. Match Play In match play if a claim is lodged with the Committee under Rule 2-5, a decision should be given as soon as possible so that the state of the match may, if necessary, be adjusted.

If a claim is not made within the time limit provided by Rule 2-5, it shall not be considered unless it is based on facts previously unknown to the player making the claim and the player making the claim had been given wrong information (Rules 6-2a and 9) by an opponent. In any case, no later claim shall be considered after the result of the match has been officially announced, unless the Committee is satisfied that the opponent knew he was giving wrong information.

b. Stroke Play Except as provided below, in stroke play no penalty shall be rescinded, modified or imposed after the competition is closed. A competition is deemed to have closed when the result has been officially announced or, in stroke play qualifying followed by match play, when the player has teed off in his first match.

A penalty of disqualification shall be imposed at any time if a competitor:

(i)   returns a score for any hole lower than actually taken (Rule 6-6d) for any reason other than failure to include a penalty which he did not know he had incurred; or

(ii) returns a score card on which he has recorded a handicap which he knows is higher than that to which he is entitled, and this affects the number of strokes received (Rule 6-2b).

34-2.   Referee's Decision
If a referee has been appointed by the Committee, his decision shall be final.

34-3.   Committee's Decision
In the absence of a referee, the players shall refer any dispute to the Committee, whose decision shall be final.

If the Committee cannot come to a decision, it shall refer the dispute to the Rules of Golf Committee of the Royal and Ancient Golf Club of St. Andrews, whose decision shall be final.

If the point in doubt or dispute has not been referred to the Rules of Golf Committee, the player or players have the right to refer an agreed statement through the Secretary of the Club to the Rules of Golf Committee for an opinion as to the correctness of the decision given. The reply will be sent to the Secretary of the Club or Clubs concerned.

If play is conducted other than in accordance with the Rules of Golf, the Rules of Golf Committee will not give a decision on any question.

Appendix I

Local Rules (Rule 33-8) and
Conditions of the Competition (Rule 33-1)

Part A   Local Rules

The Committee may make and publish Local Rules (for Specimen Local Rules see Part B) for such abnormal conditions as:

1.   Obstructions

a. General   Clarifying the status of objects which may be obstructions (Rule 24).

Declaring any construction to be an integral part of the course and accordingly, not an obstruction, e.g. built-up sides of teeing grounds, putting greens and bunkers (Rules 24 and 33-2a).

b. Stones in Bunkers   Allowing the removal of stones in bunkers by declaring them to be 'movable obstructions' (Rule 24).

c. Roads and Paths

   (i)   Declaring artificial surfaces and sides of roads and paths to be integral parts of the course, or

   (ii)   Providing relief of the type afforded under Rule 24-2b from roads and paths not having artificial surfaces and sides if they could unfairly affect play.

d. Fixed Sprinkler Heads   Providing relief from intervention by fixed sprinkler heads within two club-lengths of the putting green when the ball lies within two club-lengths of the sprinkler head.

e. Temporary Immovable Obstructions   Specimen Local Rules for application in Tournament Play are available from the Royal and Ancient Golf Club of St Andrews.

2.   Areas of the Course Requiring Preservation

Assisting preservation of the course by defining areas, including turf nurseries, young plantations and other parts of the course under cultivation, as 'ground under repair' from which play is prohibited.

3.   Unusual Damage to the Course or Accumulation of Leaves (or the like)

Declaring such areas to be 'ground under repair' (Rule 25). Note: For relief from aerification holes see Specimen Local Rule in Part B of this Appendix.

156 *Golf*

Extreme Wetness, Mud, Poor Conditions and Protection of Course

a. Lifting an Embedded Ball, Cleaning Where the ground is unusually soft, the Committee may, by temporary Local Rule, allow the lifting of a ball which is embedded in its own pitch-mark in the ground in an area 'through the green' which is not 'closely mown' (Rule 25-2) if it is satisfied that the proper playing of the game would otherwise be prevented. The Local Rule shall be for that day only or for a short period, and if practicable shall be confined to specified areas. The Committee shall withdraw the Local Rule as soon as conditions warrant and should not print it on the score card.

In similarly adverse conditions, the Committee may, by temporary Local Rule, permit the cleaning of a ball 'through the green'.

b. "Preferred Lies" and "Winter Rules" Adverse conditions, including the poor condition of the course or the existence of mud, are sometimes so general, particularly during winter months, that the Committee may decide to grant relief by temporary Local Rule either to protect the course or to promote fair and pleasant play. Such Local Rule shall be withdrawn as soon as conditions warrant.

5. Other Local Conditions which Interfere with the Proper Playing of the Game If this necessitates modification of a Rule of Golf the approval of the Governing Authority must be obtained.

Other matters which the Committee could cover by Local Rule include:

6. Water Hazards

a. Lateral Water Hazards Clarifying the status of sections of water hazards which may be lateral water hazards (Rule 26).

b. Provisional Ball Permitting play of a provisional ball for a ball which may be in a water hazard or such character that it would be impracticable to determine whether the ball is in hazard or to do so would unduly delay play. In such a case, if a provisional ball is played and the original ball is in a water hazard, the player may play the original ball as it lies or continue the provisional ball in play, but he may not proceed under Rule 26-1.

7. Defining Bounds and Margins

Specifying means used to define out of bounds, hazards, water hazards, lateral water hazards and ground under repair.

8. Dropping Zones

Establishing special areas in which balls may or shall be dropped when it is not feasible or practicable to proceed exactly in conformity with Rule 24-2b (Immovable Obstruction), Rule 25-1b or Rule 25-1c (Ground Under Repair), Rule 26-1 (Water Hazards and Lateral Water Hazards) or Rule 28 (Ball Unplayable).

9. Priority on the Course

The Committee may make regulations governing Priority on the Course (see Etiquette).

Part B.   Specimen Local Rules
Within the policy set out in Part A of this Appendix the Committee may adopt a Specimen Local Rule by referring, on a score card or notice board, to the examples given below. However Specimen Local Rules 4, 5 or 6 should not be printed or referred to on a score card as they are all of limited duration.

1.   Fixed Sprinkler Heads
All fixed sprinkler heads are immovable obstructions and relief from interference by them may be obtained under Rule 24-2. In addition, if such an obstruction on or within two club-lengths of the putting green of the hole being played intervenes on the line of play between the ball and the hole, the player may obtain relief, without penalty, as follows:

If the ball lies off the putting green but not in a hazard and is within two club-lengths of the intervening obstruction, it may be lifted, cleaned and dropped at the nearest point to where the ball lay which (a) is not nearer the hole, (b) avoids such intervention and (c) is not in a hazard or on a putting green.

PENALTY FOR BREACH OF LOCAL RULE:
Match play – Loss of hole; Stroke play – Two strokes.

2.   Stones in Bunkers
Stones in bunkers are movable obstructions. Rule 24-1 applies.

3.   Ground Under Repair: Play Prohibited
If a player's ball lies in an area of 'ground under repair' from which play is prohibited, or if such an area of 'ground under repair' interferes with the player's stance or the area of his intended swing the player must take relief under Rule 25-1.

PENALTY FOR BREACH OF LOCAL RULE:
Match play – Loss of hole; Stroke play – Two strokes.

4.   Lifting an Embedded Ball
(Specify the area if practicable) . . . through the green, a ball embedded in its own pitch-mark in ground other than sand may be lifted, cleaned and dropped, without penalty, as near as possible to the spot where it lay but not nearer the hole.

PENALTY FOR BREACH OF LOCAL RULE:
Match play – Loss of hole: Stroke play – Two strokes.

5.   Cleaning Ball
(Specify the area if practicable) . . . through the green a ball may be lifted, cleaned and replaced without penalty.

Note: The position of the ball shall be marked before it is lifted under this Local Rule – see Rule 20-1.

6.   'Preferred Lies' and 'Winter Rules'
A ball lying on any 'closely mown area' through the green may, without penalty, be moved or may be lifted, cleaned and placed within six inches of

where it originally lay, but not nearer the hole. After the ball has been so moved or placed, it is in play.

PENALTY FOR BREACH OF LOCAL RULE:
Match play – Loss of hole; Stroke play – Two strokes.

7.   Aerification Holes

If a ball comes to rest in an aerification hole, the player may, without penalty, lift the ball and clean it. Through the green, the player shall drop the ball as near as possible to where it lay, but not nearer the hole. On the putting green, the player shall place the ball at the nearest spot not nearer the hole which avoids such situation.

PENALTY FOR BREACH OF LOCAL RULE:
Match play – Loss of hole; Stroke play – Two strokes.

Part C.   Conditions of the Competition

Rule 33-1 provides, 'The Committee shall lay down the conditions under which a competition is to be played'. Such conditions should include many matters such as method of entry, eligibility, number of rounds to be played, settling ties, etc. which is not appropriate to deal with in the Rules of Golf or this Appendix.

However there are four matters which might be covered in the Conditions of the Competition to which the Committee's attention is specifically drawn by way of a Note to the appropriate Rule. These are:

1.   Specification of the Ball (Note to Rule 5-1)

Arising from the regulations for ball-testing under Rule 5-1, Lists of Conforming Golf Balls will be issued from time to time.

It is recommended that the Lists should be applied to all National and County (or equivalent) Championships and to all top class events when restricted to low handicap players. In order to apply the Lists to a particular competition the Committee must lay this down in the Conditions of the Competition. This should be referred to in the Entry Form, and also a notice should be displayed on the Club notice board and at the 1st Tee along the following lines:

.... (Name of Event) ....
.... (Date and Club) ....

The ball the player uses shall be named on the current List of Conforming Golf Balls issued by the Royal and Ancient Golf Club of St Andrews.

Note 1: A penalty statement will be required and must be either:

(a) 'PENALTY FOR BREACH OF CONDITION:
Disqualification.'

or

(b) 'PENALTY FOR BREACH OF CONDITION:
Match play – Loss of each hole at which a breach occurred: Stroke play – Two strokes for each hole at which a breach occurred.'

If option (b) is adopted this only applies to use of a ball which, whilst not on the List of Conforming Golf Balls, does conform to the specifications set forth in Rule 5 and Appendix III. The penalty for use of a ball which does not so conform is disqualification.

Note 2: In Club events it is recommended that no such condition be applied.

2. Time of Starting (Note to Rule 6-3a)
If the Committee wishes to act in accordance with the Note, the following wording is recommended:

'If, in the absence of circumstances which warrant waiving the penalty of disqualification as provided in rule 33-7, the player arrives at his starting point, ready to play, within five minutes after his starting time, the penalty for failure to start on time is loss of the first hole in match play or two strokes at the first hole in stroke play.'

3. Practice
The Committee may make regulations governing practice in accordance with the Note to Rule 7-1, Exception (c) to Rule 7-2, Note 2 to Rule 7 and Rule 33-2c.

4. Advice in Team Competitions
If the Committee wishes to act in accordance with the Note, the following wording is recommended:

'In accordance with the Note to Rule 8-1 of the Rules of Golf each team may appoint one person (in addition to the persons from whom advice may be asked under that Rule) who may give advice to members of that team. Such person [*if it is desired to insert any restriction on who may be nominated insert such restriction here*] shall be identified to the Committee prior to the start of the competition.'

Appendices II and III

Any design in a club or ball which is not covered by Rules 4 and 5 and Appendices II and III, or which might significantly change the nature of the game, will be ruled on by the Royal and Ancient Golf Club of St. Andrews and the United States Golf Association.

Note: Equipment approved for use or marketed prior to January 1st, 1984 which conformed to the Rules in effect in 1983 but does not conform to the 1984 Rules may be used until December 31st, 1989; thereafter all equipment must conform to the current Rules.

Appendix II

Design of Clubs

Rule 4-1 prescribes general regulations for the design of clubs. The following paragraphs, which provide some detailed specifications and clarify how Rule 4-1 is interpreted, should be read in conjunction with this Rule.

4-1b. Shaft

Generally Straight   The shaft shall be at least 18 inches (457 mm) in length. It shall be straight from the top of the grip to a point not more than 5 inches (127mm) above the sole, measured along the axis of the shaft and the neck or socket.

Bending and Twisting Properties   The shaft must be so designed and manufactured that at any point along its length:
    (i)   it bends in such a way that the deflection is the same regardless of how the shaft is rotated about its longitudinal axis; and
    (ii)   it twists the same amount in both directions.

Attachment to Clubhead   The neck or socket must not be more than 5 inches (127mm) in length, measured from the top of the neck or socket to the sole along its axis. The shaft and the neck or socket must remain in line with the heel, or with a point to the right or left of the heel, when the club is viewed in the address position. The distance between the axis of the shaft or the neck or socket and the back of the heel must not exceed 0.625 inches (16mm).

    Exception for Putters: The shaft or neck or socket of a putter may be fixed at any point in the head and need not remain in line with the heel. The axis of the shaft from the top to a point not more than 5 inches (127mm) above the sole must diverge from the vertical in the toe-heel plane by at least 10 degrees when the club is in its normal address position.

4-1c. Grip
    (i)   For clubs other than putters the grip must be generally circular in cross-section, except that a continuous, straight, slightly raised rib may be incorporated along the full length of the grip.
    (ii)   A putter grip may have a non-circular cross-section, provided the

cross-section has no concavity and remains generally similar throughout the length of the grip.
(iii)   The grip may be tapered but must not have any bulge or waist.
(iv)   For clubs other than putters the axis of the grip must coincide with the axis of the shaft.

4-1d.   Clubhead
Dimensions   The dimensions of a clubhead (see diagram) are measured, with the clubhead in its normal address position, on horizontal lines between vertical projections of the outermost points of (i) the heel and the toe and (ii) the face and the back. If the outermost point of the heel is not clearly defined, it is deemed to be 0.625 inches (16mm) above the horizontal plane on which the club is resting in its normal address position.
Plain in Shape   The clubhead shall be generally plain in shape. All parts shall be rigid, structural in nature and functional.

Features such as holes through the head, windows or transparencies, or appendages to the main body of the head such as plates, rods or fins for the purpose of meeting dimensional specifications, for aiming or for any other purpose are not permitted. Exceptions may be made for putters.

Any furrows in or runners on the sole shall not extend into the face.

4-1e.   Club Face
Hardness and Rigidity   The club face must not be designed and manufactured to have the effect at impact of a spring which would unduly influence the movement of the ball.
Markings   Except for specified markings, the surface roughness must not exceed that of decorative sandblasting. Markings must not have sharp edges or raised lips, as determined by a finger test. Markings within the area where impact is intended (the 'impact area') are governed by the following:
(i)   **Grooves**   A series of straight grooves with diverging sides and a symmetrical cross-section may be used. (See diagram.) The width and cross-section must be generally consistent across the face of the club and along the length of the grooves. Any rounding of groove edges shall be in the form of a radius which does not exceed 0.020 inches (0.5mm). The width of the grooves shall not exceed 0.035 inches (0.9mm), using the 30 degree method of measurement on file with the Royal and Ancient Golf Club of St. Andrews. The distance between edges of adjacent grooves must not be less than three times the width of a groove, and not less than 0.075 inches (1.9mm). The depth of a groove must not exceed 0.020 inches (0.5mm).
(ii)   **Punch Marks**   Punch marks may be used. The area of any such mark must not exceed 0.0044 square inches (2.8 sq.mm). A mark must not be closer to an adjacent mark than 0.168 inches (4.3mm) measured from centre to centre. The depth of a punch mark must not exceed 0.040 inches (1.0mm). If punch marks are used in combination with grooves, a punch mark may not be closer to a groove than 0.168 inches (4.3mm), measured from centre to centre.

Decorative Markings   The centre of the impact area may be indicated by a design within the boundary of a square whose sides are 0.375 inches (9.5mm) in length. Such a design must not unduly influence the movement of the ball. Markings outside the impact area must not be greater than 0.040 inches (1.00mm) in depth and width.

Non-metallic Club Face Markings   The above specifications for markings do not apply to non-metallic clubs with loft angles less than 24 degrees, but markings which could unduly influence the movement of the ball are prohibited. Non-metallic clubs with a loft or face angle exceeding 24 degrees may have grooves of maximum width 0.040 inches (1.0mm) and maximum depth 1½ times the groove width, but must otherwise conform to the markings specifications above.

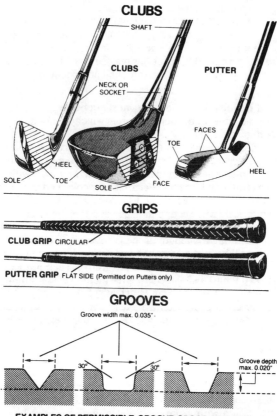

CLUBS

SHAFT

CLUBS

PUTTER

NECK OR
SOCKET

FACES

TOE

HEEL

SOLE   TOE   SOLE   FACE

HEEL

GRIPS

CLUB GRIP CIRCULAR

PUTTER GRIP FLAT SIDE (Permitted on Putters only)

GROOVES

Groove width max. 0.035".

30°   30°

Groove depth
max. 0.020"

EXAMPLES OF PERMISSIBLE GROOVE CROSS-SECTIONS

Appendix III

The Ball

a. Weight The weight of the ball shall not be greater than 1.620 ounces avoirdupois (45.93gm).

b. Size The diameter of the ball shall be not less than 1.680 inches (42.67mm). This specification will be satisfied if, under its own weight, a ball falls through a 1.680 inches diameter ring gauge in fewer than 25 out of a 100 randomly selected positions, the test being carried out at a temperature of $23 \pm 1°C$.

c. Spherical Symmetry The ball shall be designed and manufactured to perform in general as if it were spherically symmetrical.

As outlined in procedures on file at the Royal and Ancient Golf Club of St. Andrews, differences in peak angle of trajectory, carry and time of flight will be measured when 40 balls of the same type are launched, spinning 20 about one axis and 20 about another axis.

These tests will be performed using apparatus approved by the Royal and Ancient Golf Club of St. Andrews. If in two successive tests differences in the same two or more measurements are statistically significant at the 5% level of significance and exceed the limits set forth below, the ball type will not conform to the symmetry specification.

Measurement	Maximum Absolute Difference of the Means
Peak angle of trajectory	0.9 grid units (approx. 0.4 degrees)
Carry distance	2.5 yards
Flight time	0.16 seconds

Note: Methods of determining whether a ball performs as if it were generally spherically symmetrical may be subject to change as instrumentation becomes available to measure other properties accurately, such as the aerodynamic coefficient of lift, coefficient of drag and moment of inertia.

d. Initial Velocity The velocity of the ball shall not be greater than 250 feet (76.2m) per second when measured on apparatus approved by the Royal and Ancient Golf Club of St. Andrews. A maximum tolerance of 2%

will be allowed. The temperature of the ball when tested shall be 23 ± 1°C.
e. Overall Distance Standard   A brand of golf ball, when tested on apparatus approved by the Royal and Ancient Golf Club of St. Andrews under the conditions set forth in the Overall Distance Standard for golf balls on file with the Royal and Ancient Golf Club of St. Andrews, shall not cover an average distance in carry and roll exceeding 280 yards (256 metres) plus a tolerance of 6%.

Note: The 6% tolerance will be reduced to a minimum of 4% as test techniques are improved.

Notes to Appendix III
1   The size specification in (b) above will take effect from 1st January, 1990. Until that date the previous size specification of a diameter not less than 1.620 inches (41.15mm) will apply.
2   The Overall Distance Standard will apply only to balls which meet the new size specification of a diameter not less than 1.680 inches (42.67mm).
3   In international team competitions, until 31 December, 1989, the previous size specification of a diameter not less than 1.620 inches (41.15mm) will apply.

Handicaps

The Rules of Golf do not legislate for the allocation and adjustment of handicaps or their playing differentials. Such matters are within the jurisdiction and control of the National Union concerned and queries should be directed accordingly.

Rules of Amateur Status

(Effective from 1st January 1987)
as approved by The Royal and Ancient Golf Club of St. Andrews

Definition of an Amateur Golfer

An Amateur Golfer is one who plays the game as a non-remunerative or non-profit-making sport.

The Governing Body

The Governing Body of golf for the Rules of Amateur Status in any country is the National Union of the country concerned except in Great Britain and Ireland where the Governing Body is the Royal and Ancient Golf Club of St. Andrews.

Any person who considers that any action he is proposing to take might endanger his Amateur Status should submit particulars to the appropriate Committee of the Governing Body for consideration.

Rule 1.   Forfeiture of Amateur Status at any age

The following are examples of acts at any age which are contrary to the Definition of an Amateur Golfer and cause forfeiture of Amateur Status:

1.   Professionalism

a. Receiving payment or compensation for serving as a Professional golfer or a teaching or playing assistant to a Professional golfer.

b. Taking any action for the purpose of becoming a Professional golfer except applying unsuccessfully for the position of a teaching or playing assistant to a Professional golfer.

Note 1. Such actions include filing application to a school or competition conducted to qualify persons to play as professionals in tournaments; receiving services from or entering into an agreement, written or oral, with a sponsor or professional agent; agreement to accept payment or compensation for allowing one's name or likeness as a skilled golfer to be used for any commercial purpose; and holding or retaining membership in any organisation of Professional golfers.

Note 2. Receiving payment or compensation as a shop assistant is not itself a breach of the Rules, provided duties do not include playing or giving instruction.

2. Playing for Prize Money Playing for prize money or its equivalent in a match, tournament or exhibition.

3. Instruction Receiving payment or compensation for giving instruction in playing golf, either orally, in writing, by pictures or by other demonstrations, to either individuals or groups.

Exceptions:

1. Golf instruction may be given by an employee of an educational institution or system to students of the institution or system and by camp counsellors to those in their charge, provided that the total time devoted to golf instruction during a year comprises less than 50 per cent of the time spent during the year in the performance of all duties as such employee or counsellor.

2. Payment or compensation may be accepted for instruction in writing, provided one's ability or reputation as a golfer was not a major factor in his employment or in the commission or sale of his work.

4. Prizes and Testimonials

(a) Acceptance of a prize or prize voucher or retail value exceeding as follows:

	In GB & I	Elsewhere
For an event of more than 2 rounds	£170	$400 US or the equivalent
For an event of 2 rounds or less	£110	$260 US or the equivalent

or such lesser figure, if any, as may be decided by the Governing Body of golf in any country, or

(b) Acceptance of a testimonial in Great Britain and Ireland of retail value exceeding £170, elsewhere of retail value exceeding $400 US or the equivalent, or such lesser figure as may be decided by the Governing Body of golf in any country, or

(c) For a junior golfer, of such an age as may be determined by the Governing Body of golf in any country, taking part in an event limited exclusively to juniors, acceptance of a prize or prize voucher in Great Britain and Ireland of retail value exceeding £50; elsewhere of retail value exceeding $120 US or the equivalent, or such lesser figure, if any, as may be decided by the Governing Body of golf in any country, or

(d) Conversion of a prize or prize voucher into money, or

(e) Accepting a gratuity in connection with a golfing event.

Exceptions:

1. Prizes of only symbolic value, provided that their symbolic nature is distinguished by distinctive permanent marking.

2. More than one testimonial award may be accepted from different donors even though their total retail value exceeds £170 or $400 US, provided they are not presented so as to evade such value limit for a single award.

Note 1. Events covered. The limits referred to in Clauses (a) or (c) above apply to total prize or prize vouchers received by any one person for any event or series of events in any one tournament or exhibition, including hole-in-one or other events in which golf skill is a factor.

Note 2. 'Retail value' is the price at which merchandise is available to anyone at a retail source, and the onus of proving the value of a particular prize rests with the donor.

Note 3. Purpose of prize vouchers. A prize voucher may be issued and redeemed only by the Committee in charge of the competition for the purchase of goods from a Professional's shop or other retail source, which may be specified by the Committee. It may not be used for such items as travel or hotel expenses, a bar bill, or a Club subscription.

Note 4. Maximum Value of Prizes in any event for individuals. It is recommended that the total value of scratch or each division of handicap prizes should not exceed twice the maximum retail value of prize permitted in Rule 1-4(a) and (c) in an 18-hole competition, three times in a 36-hole competition four times in a 54-hole competition and five times in a 72-hole competition.

Note 5. Testimonial Awards. Such awards relate to notable performances or contributions to golf as distinguished from tournament prizes.

5. Lending Name or Likeness Because of golf skill or golf reputation receiving or contracting to receive payment, compensation or personal benefit, directly or indirectly, for allowing one's name or likeness to be used in any way for the advertisement or sale of anything, whether or not used in or appertaining to golf except as a golf author or broadcaster as permitted by Rule 1-7.

Note: A player may accept equipment from anyone dealing in such equipment provided no advertising is involved.

6. Personal Appearance Because of golf skill or golf reputation, receiving payment or compensation, directly or indirectly, for a personal appearance.

Exception:

Actual expenses in connection with personal appearances may be paid or reimbursed provided no golf competition or exhibition is involved.

7. Broadcasting and Writing Because of golf skill or golf reputation, receiving payment or compensation, directly or indirectly, for broadcasting concerning golf, a golf event or golf events, writing golf articles or books, or allowing one's name to be advertised or published as the author of golf articles or books of which he is not actually the author.

Exceptions:

1. Broadcasting or writing as part of one's primary occupation or career, provided instruction in playing golf is not included (Rule 1-3).

2. Part-time broadcasting or writing, provided (a) the player is actually the author of the commentary, articles or books, (b) instruction in playing golf is not included and (c) the payment or compensation does not have the purpose or effect, directly or indirectly, of financing participation in a golf competition or golf competitions.

8. Expenses   Accepting expenses, in money or otherwise, from any source to engage in a golf competition or exhibition.

Exceptions:

A player may receive expenses, not exceeding the actual expenses incurred, as follows:

1. From a member of the family or legal guardian;

or

2. As a player in a golf competition or exhibition limited exclusively to players who have not reached their 18th birthday;

or

3. As a representative of his Country, County, Club or similar body in team competitions or team training camps at home or abroad, or as a representative of his Country taking part in a National Championship abroad immediately preceding or following directly upon an international team competition, where such expenses are paid by the body he represents, or by the body controlling golf in the territory he is visiting;

or

4. As an individual nominated by a National or County Union or a Club to engage in an event at home or abroad provided that:

(a) The player nominated has not reached such age as may be determined by the Governing Body of Golf in the country from which the nomination is made.

(b) The expenses shall be paid only by the National Union or County Union responsible in the area from which the nomination is made and shall be limited to twenty competitive days in any one calendar year. The expenses are deemed to include reasonable travelling time and practice days in connection with the twenty competitive days.

(c) Where the event is to take place abroad, the approval of the National Union of the country in which the event is to be staged and, if the nominating body is not the National Union of the country from which the nomination is made, the approval of the National Union shall first be obtained by the nominating body.

(d) Where the event is to take place at home, and where the nomination is made by a County Union or Club, the approval of the National Union or the County Union in the area in which the event is to be staged shall first be obtained.

(*Note:* The term 'County Union' covers any Province, State or equivalent Union or Association);

or

5. As a player invited for reasons unrelated to golf skill, e.g. celebrities, business associates, etc. to take part in golfing events;

or

6. As a player in an exhibition in aid of a recognised Charity provided the exhibition is not run in connection with another golfing event.

or

7. As a player in a handicap individual or handicap team sponsored golfing event where expenses are paid by the sponsor on behalf of the player to take

part in the event provided the event has been approved as follows:
(a) where the event is to take place at home the approval of the Governing
     Body (see Definition) shall first be obtained in advance by the sponsor,
     and
(b) where the event is to take place both at home and abroad the approval
     of the two or more Governing Bodies shall first be obtained in advance
     by the sponsor. The application for this approval should be sent to the
     Governing Body of golf in the country where the competition com-
     mences.
(c) where the event is to take place abroad the approval of two or more
     Governing Bodies shall first be obtained by the sponsor. The applica-
     tion for this approval should be sent to the Governing Body of golf in
     the country whose players shall be taking part in the event abroad.
     (*Note 1:* Business Expenses. It is permissible to play in a golf competi-
     tion while on a business trip with expenses paid provided that the golf
     part of the expenses is borne personally and is not charged to business.
     Further, the business involved must be actual and substantial, and not
     merely a subterfuge for legitimising expenses when the primary pur-
     pose is a golf competition.)
     (*Note 2:* Private Transport. Acceptance of private transport furnished
     or arranged for by a tournament sponsor, directly or indirectly, as an
     inducement for a player to engage in a golf competition or exhibition
     shall be considered accepting expenses under Rule 1-8.)
9. Scholarships Because of golf skill or golf reputation, accepting
the benefits of a scholarship or grant-in-aid other than one whose terms
and conditions have been approved by the Amateur Status Committee
of the Royal and Ancient Golf Club of St. Andrews.
10. Membership Because of golf skill accepting membership in a
Golf Club without full payment for the class of membership for the
purpose of playing for that Club.
11. Conduct Detrimental to Golf Any conduct, including activities
in connection with golf gambling, which is considered detrimental to
the best interests of the game.

Rule 2. Procedure for Enforcement and Reinstatement
1. Decision on a Breach Whenever information of a possible act
contrary to the Definition of an Amateur Golfer by a player claiming to
be an Amateur shall come to the attention of the appropriate Committee of the Governing Body, the Committee, after such investigation as
it may deem desirable, shall decide whether a breach has occurred.
Each case shall be considered on its merits. The decision of the
Committee shall be final.
2. Enforcement Upon a decision that a player has acted contrary to
the Definition of an Amateur Golfer, the Committee may declare the
Amateur Status of the player forfeited or require the player to refrain
or desist from specified actions as a condition of retaining his Amateur
Status.

The Committee shall use its best endeavours to ensure that the player is notified and may notify any interested Golf Association of any action taken under this paragraph.

3. Reinstatement The Committee shall have sole power to reinstate a player to Amateur Status or to deny reinstatement. Each application for reinstatement shall be decided on its merits. In considering an application for reinstatement, the Committee shall normally be guided by the following principles:

a. Awaiting Reinstatement The professional holds an advantage over the Amateur by reason of having devoted himself to the game as his profession; other persons infringing the Rules of Amateur Status also obtain advantages not available to the amateur. They do not necessarily lose such advantage merely by deciding to cease infringing the Rules. Therefore, an applicant for reinstatement to Amateur Status shall undergo a period awaiting reinstatement as prescribed by the Committee.

The period awaiting reinstatement shall start from the date of the player's last breach of the Definition of an Amateur Golfer unless the Committee decides that it shall start from the date when the player's last breach became known to the Committee.

b. Period Awaiting Reinstatement The period awaiting reinstatement shall normally be related to the period the player was in breach. However, no applicant shall normally be eligible for reinstatement until he has conducted himself in accordance with the Definition of an Amateur Golfer for a period of at least two consecutive years. The Committee, however, reserves the right to extend or to shorten such a period. A longer period will normally be required of applicants who have been in breach for more than five years. Players of national prominence who have been in breach for more than five years shall not normally be eligible for reinstatement.

c. One Reinstatement A player shall not normally be reinstated more than once.

d. Status While Awaiting Reinstatement During the period awaiting reinstatement an applicant for reinstatement shall conform with the Definition of an Amateur Golfer.

He shall not be eligible to enter competitions as an Amateur. He may, however, enter competitions, and win a prize, solely among members of a Club of which he is a member, subject to the approval of the Club; but he may not represent such Club against other Clubs.

Forms of Application for Countries under the Jurisdiction of the Royal and Ancient Golf Club

(a) Each application for reinstatement shall be submitted on the approved form to the County Union where the applicant wishes to play as an Amateur. Such Union shall, after making all necessary enquiries, forward it through the National Union (and in the case of lady applicants, the Ladies' Golf Union) and the appropriate Professional

Golfers' Association, with comments endorsed thereon, to the Governing Body of golf in that country. Forms of application for reinstatement may be obtained from the Royal and Ancient Golf Club or from the National or County Unions. The application shall include such information as the Royal and Ancient Golf Club may require from time to time and it shall be signed and certified by the applicant.

(b) Any application made in countries under the jurisdiction of the Royal and Ancient Golf Club of St. Andrews which the Governing Body of golf in that country considers to be doubtful or not to be covered by the above regulations may be submitted to the Royal and Ancient Golf Club of St. Andrews whose decision shall be final.

R. & A. Policy on Gambling

The Definition of an Amateur Golfer provides that an Amateur golfer is one who plays the game as a non-remunerative or non-profit-making sport. When gambling motives are introduced, evils can arise which threaten the integrity both of the game and of the individual players.

The R&A does not object to participation in wagering among individual golfers or teams of golfers when participation in the wagering is limited to the players, the players may only wager on themselves or their teams, the sole source of all money won by players is advanced by the players and the primary purpose is the playing of the game for enjoyment.

The distinction between playing for prize money and gambling is essential to the validity of the Rules of Amateur Status. The following constitute golf wagering and not playing for prize money:

1. Participation in wagering among individual golfers.

2. Participation in wagering among teams.

Organised Amateur events open to the general golfing public and designed and promoted to create cash prizes are not approved by the R&A. Golfers participating in such events without irrevocably waiving their right to cash prizes are deemed by the R&A to be playing for prize money.

The R&A is opposed to and urges Unions and Clubs and all other sponsors of golf competitions to prohibit types of gambling such as: Calcuttas, auction sweepstakes and any other forms of gambling organised for general participation or permitting participants to bet on someone other than themselves or their teams.

Attention is drawn to Rule 1-11 relating to conduct detrimental to the game, under which players can forfeit their amateur status. It is the Club which, by permitting competitions where excessive gambling is involved, or illegal prizes are offered, bears the responsibility for which the individual is penalised, and Unions have the power to invoke severe sanctions against a Club or individual for consistently ignoring this policy.

Index
to the Rules of Golf

Rule

Rule

Rule

Rule

Rule

Rule

	Rule